edexcel
advancing learning, changing lives

Edexcel AS History Unit 1

The Collapse of the Liberal State and the Triumph of Fascism in Italy, 1896–1943

Andrew Mitchell and Geoff Stewart

Series editors: Derrick Murphy and Angela Leonard

STUDENT BOOK

A PEARSON COMPANY

Contents

Introduction

Welcome to History at AS level. History is a fascinating subject, concerned with the world as it was and how it became the world we know now. By studying history, you will encounter new people, new places, new societies and cultures – even though they are all in the past. If you have an enquiring mind and an interest in the world around you then History is the subject for you.

How to make the most of the course

- Practise your skills. History is not just about learning information or about telling the story of what happened in the past. You need to be able to understand and explain why things turned out the way they did and about how much they changed. The Skills Builder sections in this book will help you do this.
- Prepare for debate and discussion. Historians do not always agree about why events or developments in the past happened, or about their importance – so don't be afraid to debate with your teacher and other students. But remember that you must give evidence to support any point you make.
- Use the course book. This book has been designed to help you build up the skills, knowledge and understanding to help you do well in your exam – so use it. See the 'How this book will help you' section overleaf for details.
- Read around the subject. The more you learn about a period of history, the more interesting it becomes. Further reading on your chosen topics will broaden your understanding of the period, give you better insights into causation and change, and make the course much more rewarding.

What you will learn

Unit 1 focuses on historical themes in breadth. This means that you need to be able to understand and explain why things changed over a fairly long period. In Option E3/F3 you will focus on Italy and the way in which a limited liberal democracy faced serious challenges which eventually destroyed it. First, you will consider the nature of Italian society, economy and the political system that had emerged from unification in the middle years of the nineteenth century. How far could Italy be considered one of the great powers of Europe? Second, you will consider the immediate impact of the First World War in the years 1915–18 and the post-war crisis that emerged between 1918 and 1922. Third, you will examine the nature of the Fascist regime that came to power in 1922 and evolved into a dictatorship in the later 1920s. How did it achieve this and how did it seek to hold on to power and transform Italy? Finally, you will study Mussolini's attempt to make Italy a truly great power in Europe and try to assess how far he had succeeded in the 1930s and why and how disaster struck in the early 1940s.

How you will be assessed

For Unit 1 you will take a written exam. You will write two essays: one on each topic you have studied (i.e. one on Italy 1896–1943 and one on your other chosen topic). For each topic you will have a choice of two questions. You will have 1 hour and 20 minutes in total, or 40 minutes for each essay.

How this book will help you

- Clearly written text gives you the historical information you need for this topic in the right amount of depth.
- 'Take note' boxes indicate when you should make notes of your own. These notes will help you with the activities and can also form the basis of your revision, so it's worth keeping up to date with these as you go.
- Activities help you understand the content and build up your skills.
- Skills Builder sections help you develop the essential skills you need to do well in your exam.
- Examzone tells you what you need to know to prepare for the exam, including:
  - what to expect on the day
  - how to revise
  - what the assessment objectives mean and how you can meet them
  - what the different levels mean and how you can gain a high mark
  - example essay with examiner commentaries to help you understand what the examiners are looking for and how to use your information.

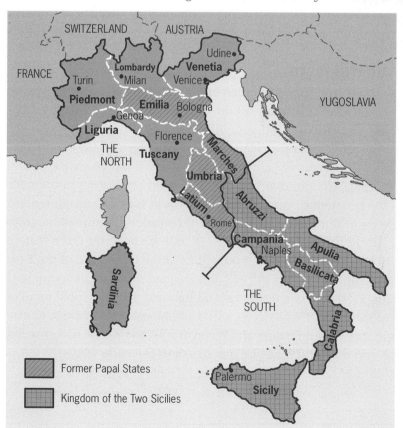

Map of the regions of Italy, 1895

Chapter 1 **Italy in 1896**

Key questions

- What was the level of economic development in late nineteenth century Italy?
- How was Italy governed?
- How unified was Italy?
- How far could Italy be considered a 'great power'?

In 1896, Puccini's masterpiece *La Boheme* was performed for the first time in Turin. In March of the same year an Italian army was bloodily defeated in Abyssinia. Italy was a cultural giant and yet a pygmy in world politics. Italy's capital was the old heart of Europe's mightiest empire, Rome, and it was within Italy that modern urban civilisation developed. European states of the sixteenth to eighteenth centuries competed for Italian scholars, artists and craftsmen to excite their courts. It was also the home of the new culinary delight, ice cream. Young Britons felt that their education was incomplete without a tour of this birthplace of Europe's culture.

Yet Italy had only become a united country in the 1860s and many problems still remained. Italy was largely agricultural and had not developed the industries that enriched its northern neighbours. It was over-populated and could barely feed its people. Every year thousands left to settle in the USA, Argentina or French North Africa. Italy had no imperial possessions before 1890 and this upset many educated Italians, who had a sense of faded glory. This new country also showed the fault lines of its divided past. The royal family from the House of Savoy preferred speaking French to Italian. The great city of Venice had closer ties with Vienna and Austria than it had with Rome. The pope refused to recognise the country which had deprived him of his lands. The South was poverty stricken and alienated from the new Italy with which it could not for the most part identify. The new kingdom clearly had a past to celebrate but it was not clear if it had a viable future.

Timeline	
1870	**Unification of Italy** completed by the capture of Rome
1882	Electoral reform; Italy joins Austria and Germany to create the Triple Alliance
1886	Pope forbids Catholics from standing or voting in parliamentary elections
1887	Wheat tariff introduced
1888	Three years' schooling becomes compulsory
1896	Defeat of Italian army at Adowa; Crispi resigns as prime minister
1896-98	Antonio Starabba prime minister

Society and economy

Italy was poor and economically backward compared to Britain, France and the new Germany. Income per head was under £8 a year in Italy, while it was £26 per head in France and £31 per head in Britain. Agricultural labourers – the commonest occupation amongst Italy's population of 30 million – earned under the equivalent of 50p a week on which to keep their often large families.

Take note

As you read through this chapter, take notes to answer these questions:
- In what ways was Italy economically backward compared to Britain, France and Germany?
- Why had Italy not developed economically as fast as Britain, France and Germany? What was holding it back?
- What regional differences were apparent?

Unification of Italy

In 1815, the Congress of Vienna divided the Italian peninsula into five major states – Piedmont, Lombardy-Venetia, Tuscany, The Papal States and the Kingdom of the Two Sicilies – and some minor ones (see map on page 4).

Italian unification was forged by the kingdom of Piedmont in the 1860s by both force and diplomacy. Previously, the area had been divided and fought over by the other European powers. Lombardy and Venetia had long been under Austrian rule, and the kings of Piedmont and the Two Sicilies had close ties to competing French royal lines.

In 1870, the unification was completed by the capture of Rome from the papacy.

Glossary

Risorgimento

The resurgence, or Italy rising up again, is the term used to describe the process of unification between 1859 and 1870. Its central characters – who became Italian heroes – were Mazzini the prophet, who had long campaigned and written about the need for unification; Cavour the practical politician, who schemed to bring it about; and Garibaldi the romantic soldier. Victor Emmanuel, the first king of Italy, was adopted as the official embodiment of unification and his monuments are to be found across the country.

Nearly 60% of the population were engaged in agriculture, compared to 10% in Britain. There were, however, enormous variations in the patterns of agriculture practised. Small-scale peasant agriculture predominated in the Alpine north but, on the rich plains of the Po Valley, there were large-scale rice or dairy farms run by their hereditary noble landowners. Sometimes these were leased on long leases to skilled professionals, who also employed labourers on a vast scale. In Tuscany and central Italy, sharecropping was the norm, with the land given out by its aristocratic owners to peasant farmers who surrendered half their crops for rent. The area to the south of Rome, Campagna, was dominated by vast estates owned by the Roman aristocracy and either sub-let or farmed by labourers. Further south was a mixture of estates, either formerly owned by the Church or by the many titled nobles, and tiny plots in the sun-burned hills farmed by poverty-stricken peasants.

Throughout Italy, former Church lands seized by the state at the time of the ***Risorgimento***, and some common or manorial land taken over by the state as feudal laws were abolished, had passed into the hands of a new type of middle-class landowners. These were often lawyers or government officials connected to local government. The local mayor and his relatives tended to enrich themselves and the half-hearted attempt to create a widespread network of independent peasant farmers was stillborn. Italian unification may have challenged the power of the traditional aristocracy but they remained powerful and now simply shared landed wealth with a new middle-class elite, who had enriched themselves through the opportunities thrown up by change.

The lives of the poor

The lives of most of Italy's agricultural workers at the end of the nineteenth century tended to be 'nasty, brutish and short'. Malaria cursed much of the south and the area around Rome; it killed 15,000 people annually and up to two million were affected by the disease. In the North, a poor diet based on *polenta* (a flour made from maize) produced vitamin deficiencies and the terrible disease pellagra, which led to insanity and death. A diet of bread and beans predominated in the South. Tomatoes, cheese and ham were luxuries few could afford and, despite the vast amount of wine produced, most went either for export or to the small middle class. Poor Italians made do with *vinello*, essentially water flavoured with the by-products of wine-making. Water itself was often infected and cholera killed thousands.

Even in death there was no dignity. In many parts of the South, corpses were simply thrown over cliffs or left in open pits for the crows to feed on. Where burials did occur, they were often in shallow graves and dogs feasted on the corpses. Houses were simple and primitive. In the South, widespread brigandage had led to large numbers living away from their fields. Instead they banded together in hill-top towns for safety, in one- or two-room houses which they shared with their animals. The really poor had no animals. Even in the North, rural houses tended to be mud huts with straw roofs and earthen floors. Perhaps the best housing was provided in Tuscany by landlords for their sharecropping tenants.

Economic crisis

In the late nineteenth century world food prices collapsed. Cheap wheat from the USA, Canada and Russia drove prices down in the 1870s and 1880s, hurting Italian farmers and leading to a demand for protective **tariffs**. The price of land fell in Sicily by 40%. In 1887 a wheat tariff was introduced and then increased, reaching 75 lire per ton by 1894. The consequences were largely disastrous. It increased the price of bread for the poor and produced a tariff war with France, which cut exports to that country of a whole range of agricultural products. The result of all this was an explosion of rural misery whose most obvious outcome was the flood of emigrants to the USA and Argentina. Already by 1891 there were nearly 1.5 million Italians living in America. Initially most emigrants had come from the north but by the 1890s 60% were from the south.

Industry

Italy had a strong craft tradition going back centuries, but the development of modern mass production in factories was held up by the lack of coal for steam power, which drove factories in Britain and Germany. The most important industry was textiles, with silk as the dominant material. This was based in the north, in Lombardy, and Italian silk production was second only to that of China. Cotton and fine woollens were also made but, as with the silk industry, these were still heavily dependent on hand-looms rather than mass factory production, although this was increasing in the 1890s.

An iron industry was developing using imported coal, stimulated by the building of railways and a large navy in the 1880s. The Terni iron and steel works was founded in 1886 and appeared an example of modern technology, but it was heavily dependent on government contracts for the navy and was not very efficient. Railways were rapidly expanded and the length of track doubled between 1870 and 1890 to 13,600 kilometres. However, railway coverage was still some way behind that of Britain, France and Germany.

In the 1880s perhaps 2–2.5 million men were involved in industry, a quarter in the building trades and the bulk of the rest in textiles, furniture and food production. Nearly 2 million women were also engaged in the production of goods, but these were not necessarily fully employed industrial workers. Unlike her northern neighbours, Italy had not really developed a mass factory-based working class. Most production remained centred in small workshops and even workers' homes.

The middle and upper classes

The old ruling elite of Italy was made up of 7387 noble families. Princes and dukes were ten-a-penny compared to Britain. There were 208 princes in Sicily alone. Very few of the Italian nobility could match the wealth of the far fewer English and Scottish aristocracy. The grand titles of many of these Italian families concealed penury, and service as an officer in the Italian army was a financial relief for many aristocrats (although junior officers' salaries were often meagre). A few still owned considerable estates or showed enterprise in developing quality wine production, such as the Ricasoli family in Tuscany.

Glossary

Liberal

A new word from the early nineteenth century, it literally means those who favoured freedom. In Italy it came to be associated with those favouring national unification and opposition to absolute royal power and the influence of the papacy. Liberals came in all shapes and sizes, from moderate constitutional monarchists like Cavour to out-and-out republicans like Mazzini.

Biography

Pope Pius IX

1792–1878

Pope from 1846 until his death in 1878, Pius began as a liberal, releasing political prisoners, but became more conservative with age. He issued the 'Syllabus of Errors' in 1864, condemning much of contemporary thought, and embraced the doctrine of papal infallibility in 1869. Pius was totally opposed to the new Italy, remaining shut away in the Vatican in protest after 1870.

There were around 200,000 landowners and business men throughout the country and it was with these that the old nobility now had to share power. In addition there were approximately 250,000 non-manual government employees, including 75,000 schoolteachers. These earned around £50 a year. Government employment was highly valued if not highly paid. It was secure and the next best thing to income from property. In addition to these publically employed members of the middle class, there were perhaps 100,000 in the professions, such as the law and medicine. A village doctor might earn about £100 per year and was likely to be a pillar of the local community. Lawyers and doctors might also be local landowners and usually dominated town government. All these members of the middle and upper classes, possibly half a million in total, formed the bedrock of the new state.

The political system

'Liberal' Italy

The new state of Italy that had emerged in the 1860s represented a triumph for **liberals**. The old forces of traditional authority – the ruling families of the different states, the old aristocracy and, above all, the pope – had been defeated. The name usually given to Italy's system of government in the 60 years after 1870 – the 'Liberal state' – emphasises this triumph. **Pope Pius IX**'s self-imposed imprisonment in the Vatican seemed to symbolise this.

Yet it was a rather conservative version of liberalism which had triumphed. The new Italy was a monarchy, not a republic as envisaged by the heroes of the *Risorgimento*. One royal family had replaced all the others. The House of Savoy, the ruling family of Piedmont, were now kings of all Italy and in some ways Italian unification was the conquest of Italy by Piedmont.

Although the new state was liberal, traditions of royal authoritarianism lived on in the new united Italy. The king exercised real power. He was head of the army in more than a nominal fashion and expected to play a major role in foreign policy. He selected the prime minister and individual ministers had to be acceptable to him. Two things limited royal authority: the need to command a majority in parliament to vote for taxes to pay for the army and government, and the character of the king. In 1896 the ruler was Umberto I, a rather insubstantial figurehead of limited intellect. He was a serial adulterer despite having a beautiful and talented queen, who was the greatest asset of the monarchy. Despite his intellectual limitations, Umberto did exercise a decisive influence on government from time to time. He pushed for the **Triple Alliance** with Germany and Austria, against republican France, and in 1898 was responsible for appointing a general as prime minister, Luigi Pelloux (see page 24).

The army was not only a prop to royal authority but a crucial national institution. It was vital in holding the new country together, sometimes by the use of force. It also drilled a sense of Italian nationalism and a common language into recruits who spoke local dialects and had little sense of national identity. The peacetime army numbered 215,000 conscripts serving for three years after their twentieth birthday. Usually only a third of those liable to serve were called up. Many were rejected as physically unfit and elder sons were left to help in keeping the family. There were 15,000 officers, the majority of whom were from Piedmont and were therefore crucial in keeping the army loyal to the House of Savoy.

Throughout much of Italy there was little popular enthusiasm for the unprepossessing king. The dominant politician of the 1880s and early 1890s, **Francesco Crispi**, contrasted Italy with Britain in a speech to parliament. 'In Britain, respect for the monarch and religious sentiment are so deeply rooted in the hearts of the people that nobody dares to insult them or puts up with their being insulted. Every meeting ends with the celebrated anthem "God save the Queen".' Crispi argued for limiting political liberty in Italy because there was little respect for the monarchy there. Originally, he had been a follower of Garibaldi and an opponent of monarchy. However, he had come to accept the monarchy as a necessary agent of unity in a deeply divided Italy lacking any traditions of national solidarity.

Biography

Francesco Crispi

1819–1901

A Sicilian who saw the monarchy as the institution that divided Italy the least, and therefore necessary to unity, Crispi was a fervent patriot and Italian nationalist. He felt that a glorious war was necessary for Italian self-respect and to create a national identity. In some ways he was a forerunner of Mussolini. He was charismatic and, although a democrat in theory, was increasingly authoritarian in practice. His hold on power was broken by the debacle of the Battle of Adowa (see page 12), for which he deserves much of the blame for pushing the Italian commander into fighting.

Parliament and 'trasformismo'

In parliament, the lack of clear political parties was partly the result of this same lack of a strong national tradition. Politicians were linked by family and local interests rather than by broadly shared political principles which stretched across the nation. This had the effect of enhancing the king's influence and gave room for intrigue and manoeuvre, allowing his favoured or prime minister to manipulate groups of politicians in support of a chosen ministry. The system became known as '**trasformismo**'. The king appointed a prime minister who juggled interests and government patronage to ensure a working majority in parliament. Towns could receive a railway link in return for the local MP's support of the government. MPs could receive an official appointment for themselves or their relatives. Government contracts and leases could be used to buy votes. Self- and family-interest predominated. Self-serving corruption was endemic and never really questioned. Parliament became the object of popular contempt and was not perceived as voicing public opinion. This was partly because there was no such thing on most issues. As a British diplomat in the Rome Embassy pointed out in 1893, high-sounding speeches about patriotism and criticism of the monarchy and parliament were rather unconvincing in a country where the non-payment of taxes was normal and favours for friends and family expected as a right in return for political support.

Glossary

Triple Alliance

This was a defensive military alliance, largely developed on the initiative of Bismarck, the German chancellor. He allied the new German Reich with the Empire of Austria-Hungary in 1879 and in 1882 persuaded the Italian government, who resented the French occupation of Tunis in that year, to join. Bismarck had encouraged the French to seize Tunis.

Trasformismo

Key concept used to describe the political system of Italy in the late nineteenth century and early twentieth century. It was the process by which governments secured majorities from amongst the different factions and groupings in parliament by bribery and exercising pressure through the prefects on local government. It was necessary in a country which had not evolved nationwide political parties.

King Umberto I in 1900

Take note

Once you have read this section, write out in your own words a definition of *trasformismo*. Summarise its strengths and weaknesses.

In addition to the Chamber of Deputies – the lower house of parliament – there was the Senate of nominated life peers. These were appointed by the prime minister, acting on behalf of the king, theoretically from amongst the great and the good. It seldom opposed the will of the government and, anyway, could always be swamped by new members if they blocked some legislation the government regarded as vital.

The crucial officials in making the whole system of government work were the prefects in charge of the 69 provinces into which Italy was divided. These officials were appointed by the government and in theory the whole local government of Italy was highly centralised. The basic unit of local government was the commune or township of which there were 8382. Each commune had an elected council headed by the mayor. The chief paid official of the town council, the town clerk, was a civil servant and as such an employee of the central government. Councils who proved troublesome or unco-operative with the government in Rome could be removed.

In practice there was a fair degree of autonomy. Local town government depended on local notables, with whom the prefect had to co-operate. The prefect's most important job was to secure the 'right' candidate won in elections to parliament and this required the co-operation of local councils and mayors. To sack one mayor or group of councillors merely put the prefect in the hands of a rival faction or family grouping. Bribery and conciliation was a more effective way of oiling the wheels of government than bullying. There were not enough Piedmontese officials to govern the whole country and the army was there merely as a last resort.

The power and influence of the papacy

The vast majority of the Italian population were Roman Catholics. The head of the Roman Catholic Church is the pope. However, the papacy was opposed to the Liberal state, which had eroded the **Papal States** until only the **Vatican City** remained. As the head of a large international organisation, the pope refused to become merely 'the chaplain of the House of Savoy' – believing that an independent state was essential to maintain the independence of the Church. He also feared that a 'Liberal' Italy would be anti-religious in its education and moral policies, for example in its attitude to divorce. In 1874 Pius IX made it clear to Catholics that they should not vote in the election of that year. His successor made the prohibition even more definite in 1886 with a decree '*non expedit prohibitionem importat*', forbidding Catholics to stand or vote in parliamentary elections. As a result turn out was poor. Good Roman Catholics were not to take part in the politics of the hated new state.

The North–South divide

A central feature of the new Italian state was the sharp contrast between northern and southern Italy, i.e. the area to the south of Rome that had been ruled from Naples by the Bourbon family before unification. The South was poverty-stricken and alienated.

Glossary

The Papal States

Before unification, the pope had been the independent ruler of a large block of territory in central Italy. All of this was lost in 1861 except the city of Rome, which was lost in 1870. The pope believed that an independent papal state was a necessary pre-condition for an independent Church.

Vatican City

The Vatican City is an enclave of Rome from where the pope traditionally ruled the Church and Papal States. Now all that is left of the pope's territory, the Vatican City is still recognised as an independent state by the international community.

People in the South found it difficult to identify with the new Italy. It was said that the best Italian was spoken around Florence in Tuscany; such Italian was barely intelligible to the peasants of Basilicata and Calabria in the South, whose mountains had once teemed with brigands and bandits. The great island of Sicily, also part of the old portion of Bourbon Italy, was even more distinctive and, if anything, even more lawless.

To many in the South, unification meant conquest by Piedmont. In the immediate aftermath of unification, a bitter **civil war** had been fought in the South. Although this was officially described by the new Italian government as a war against brigands, it was in many respects the crushing of a liberation movement by the northern army. Certainly it left a legacy of bitterness and the new Italy began its life with fresh, deep wounds.

Unification brought higher taxes and more intense conscription to the South. It was no accident that the rebels in Pontelandolfo attacked the tax collector and burnt the birth records in the church to prevent conscription. The new state of Italy seemed much more heavy-handed to the South than the backward, inefficient Bourbon state it replaced. Mules and donkeys were more heavily taxed in Sicily than the cattle of the great landowners. The new state, in other words, conciliated and accommodated the elite but repressed the masses.

The South seemed startlingly different to visitors, more backward and poor. Unintelligible dialects were spoken, certainly not the Italian of educated Tuscans. In Naples, the greatest city of the South, there were just five bookshops in 1881. Florence and Turin, both smaller in population, had more than twice as many. As the franchise was based on literacy after 1882, the educational divide between North and South had great political implications. In 1881, the illiteracy rate in Piedmont and Lombardy was roughly a third of the population. Throughout most of the South it was over 80%. In 1888, three years of schooling became compulsory throughout Italy but in much of the South this had little impact. Truancy was usually around 80%. Local councils could see nothing to be gained by enforcement and parents were largely hostile. A sullen and resentful population rejected much of the modern world and saw the concept of Italy, if they thought about it at all, as just an excuse for oppression used by the latest of many invaders and conquerors.

In 1882 the franchise was extended to all men (over 21) who were literate. This created a theoretical electorate of about 2 million, 7% of the population. Many, however, did not vote. In the South, where illiteracy was common, there were far smaller electorates than in the North. 5.5% of the population had the vote compared to 8.2% in the North. The gap grew. In 1895, the North had 56% of the total electorate and the South 26%. Yet the South, with Sicily and Sardinia, returned 203 MPs out of 508. The South was particularly vital in making *trasformismo* work and the southern political elite became adept at enriching themselves in the process. In other words, ministries relied heavily on the support of deputies from the South who could be more easily bribed, cajoled or manipulated into supporting the government, than could those in the North with a larger electorate.

The civil war, 1861–1865

Fighting started around the small town of Pontelandolfo, near Benevento. Government soldiers were killed as was the local tax collector. The result was a massacre of the inhabitants by northern troops. 400 were killed and the town burned to the ground. Fighting spread and continued until 1865, by which time over 100,000 soldiers were engaged in holding down the South. The official casualty list cites the figure of 5200 killed by the army but many estimates place it much higher. One even suggests that the victims totalled 150,000.

Take note

Look carefully at the map on page 4 and make sure you clearly understand what is meant by the South. Then, using this chapter, identify the differences which distinguished the South from the North: you could use the following headings – politics, culture, unification, economy.

Take note

What factors weakened
Italy as a great power?
Why could it not compete
with the likes of Britain and
France?

Italy as a great power

Francesco Crispi, prime minister from 1887 to 1891 and again from 1893 to 1896, was determined that Italy should play the part of a great power. He was hostile to France and a supporter of the Triple Alliance with Germany and Austria. He carried Italy into agreements with Britain, known as the Mediterranean Agreements, which essentially meant opposing Russian and French attempts to change the status quo in the Balkans and Mediterranean. In his first term as prime minister he seems to have positively desired a war with France in alliance with Germany. Luckily for the peace of Europe, France refused to be provoked. The Italian fleet was more than doubled in tonnage in the 1880s so that, by 1890, it could rival the French fleet in size if not in efficiency.

The British naval commanders in the Mediterranean had little enthusiasm for their potential allies under the Mediterranean Agreements, always hoping that, if conflict broke out between Britain and France, Italy would be neutral rather than a British ally. It was felt that Italy could be more of a military liability than an asset.

In reality, although Italy played her part in the diplomatic dances between the great powers, she was always a marginal member of the great power club. She lacked the economic muscle of the other members and had the lowest population. However, in other areas the discrepancies were far greater – as the table for 1890 below indicates. All the great European powers had acquired imperial possessions outside Europe. Britain appeared the leader in this respect, vying with Russia for control of Asia and with France for dominance in Africa. Germany had entered the race for empire late but had managed to acquire some territory in Africa in 1885–86. Italy's weaknesses were glaringly displayed when an Italian army of 17,700 was defeated by a much larger Abyssinian army on 1 March 1896. 4600 Italian troops and 289 officers were killed at Adowa. Most of the dead and some of the living prisoners were castrated. It was a terrible humiliation which the Italians could not avenge. Italy was the only European power to be defeated in this way in the process of empire building. Far from acquiring the empire Crispi sought, Italy exposed her weakness to the world.

Country	Population	Iron/steel (million tons)	Energy consumption (million tons of coal equivalent)
Britain	37.4	8.0	145
Germany	49.2	4.1	71
Russia	116.8	0.95	10.9
France	38.3	1.9	36
Austria/Hungary	42.6	0.97	19.7
Italy	30	0.01	4.5

The great powers in 1890

Conclusion: How united was the united Italy?

The newly unified Italy faced many economic, social and political problems. Economically it had not developed as its northern neighbours had and remained an overwhelmingly agricultural society. The South was particularly undeveloped. There was a very limited national consciousness outside the small middle class. The heads of state, Italy's kings drawn from the House of Savoy, elicited little enthusiasm. The pope, who still had a large following as the spiritual head of the national religion, sulked in the Vatican and would not recognise the new state. Large parts of the South were sullen and resentful, seeing unification as conquest by Savoy. To many politicians there was insufficient national pride and politics was simply an opportunity to advance family, friends and city.

> ### Taking it further
> Try to find out more about the *Risorgimento* and in particular the roles of Cavour, Mazzini and Garibaldi. What signs can you see during this period of the problems to come?

Activities: Letters of state

Write a letter as prime minister to a prefect suggesting how he might ensure that the chief towns in his area vote for government supporters.

Write a letter from the pope to a bishop, justifying why good Catholics should not recognise the state of Italy and should abstain from voting.

Activity: The challenges of 1896

Use your notes on this chapter to write a summary of the main issues that faced Italy's new prime minister and his government in the summer of 1896. Include a list of challenges and recommended courses of action to deal with the coming storm.

Chapter 2 Forces for change: Italy 1896–1914

Key questions
- How was Italy changing economically between 1896 and 1914?
- How far did the growth of socialism threaten the political system?
- How far did the Roman Catholic Church enter into politics?
- How far was rising nationalism a problem?

Between 1896 and 1914, Italy at long last began to catch up with the rest of Western Europe, putting on a spurt of economic growth that is often referred to as an economic miracle. The reasons for this are many and varied. This economic growth had both positive and negative effects. It increased government revenue and ultimately raised living standards but, in the short term, increased the numbers of workers living in crowded cities and more open to revolutionary ideas. In this sense it increased political instability. It also widened the North–South divide.

Timeline	
1891	First Italian sugar refinery set up
1893	Local government franchise widened
1894	Roman Catholic Church adopts the Milan Programme on social issues
1895	Socialist party of Turati becomes the Italian Socialist Party (PSI)
1897	Government crack down on Catholic political and social activists
1898	50,000 kilowatts of hydroelectric power produced
1899	FIAT established in Turin
1904	General strike
1907	71 car manufacturers operating in Italy
1908	Olivetti typewriter production starts
1910	41 sugar refineries operating
1912	FIAT begin production of cheap mass-produced cars
1914	1 million kilowatts of hydroelectric power produced

Take note

As you read through this section, consider why the Italian economy developed more rapidly in these years. Make a table of factors which encouraged development, and include examples of how each factor stimulated development.

Economic change

The rapid economic development in this period was the result of the interplay of various factors: technological developments, better access to long-term credit, international changes and government policies.

Credit and the currency

After the old system crashed in 1893–94, an improved banking system evolved in Italy. New banks were established with improved practices. One of the most important drew on German and Austrian capital – the *Banca Commerciale Italiana*. Like many of the new banks, this channelled money into industrial ventures and promoted new technology. The *Banca Commerciale Italiana* was particularly prominent in the development of the electrical industry.

In 1893, Prime Minister **Giovanni Giolitti** founded the Bank of Italy. This helped to develop a sound banking system as it managed the currency and acted as a **lender of last resort** to support other banks.

The state also contributed to economic success by adopting a sound attitude to government expenditure and a balanced state budget. Public spending was cut by **Sidney Sonnino**, minister of finance 1894–96. He got rid of the government deficit by raising taxes on raw materials and cutting spending and, by 1899, there was an annual budget surplus which remained until 1910. There was an impression of sound management and investors' confidence grew.

Biography

Sidney Sonnino

(1847–1922)

Born in Pisa to a Jewish Italian father and a Welsh mother, Sonnino was brought up as an Anglican Protestant. He served under Crispi as minister of finance, then served briefly as prime minister in 1906 and 1909–10. At the outbreak of the First World War, he was a supporter of the Central Powers. After becoming foreign minister in November 1914, he switched his allegiance to the Entente. With Salandra, he negotiated the 1915 Treaty of London which secured Italian intervention for the Allied cause. Sonnino was disappointed with the results of the Paris Peace Conference and retired from politics in 1919.

The currency remained stable at roughly 5 lire to the dollar and 25 lire to the pound sterling, encouraging foreign investors. This was despite a constant **trade deficit**, due in part to rapidly rising imports of coal and steel. The lire avoided being devalued because of the constant flood of foreign earnings into Italy from emigrants to the USA and Argentina. These sent home support for relatives or bought property totalling 300 million lire a year.

Power and production

The development of hydroelectric power in the alpine valleys was vital in freeing Italy from its total dependence on expensive imported coal. Coal continued to be imported and imports actually grew in these years from 4 million tons a year to 11 million tons. Nevertheless, there was a massive surge in the use of electric power generated by water. In the 1890s the distribution of power had been mastered and, in 1898, 50,000 kilowatts were generated. By 1914 this had risen to one million kilowatts and Italy was firmly amongst the leaders in this new electrical technology. Electric power assisted the development of steel production, which grew from 140,000 tons in 1900 to 930,000 tons in 1913. The Terni plant became the biggest steel plant in the world to be dependent on hydroelectric power.

Government policy played a role in stimulating development. Tariffs protected Italian production and government orders for ships and railways encouraged the development of iron and steel. Engineering was also stimulated by the ordering of 1000 locomotives between 1905 and 1908 and thousands of trucks and carriages for the state-owned railways. In the 1880s most of these had been imported but now they were home produced.

Biography

Giovanni Giolitti

(1842–1928)

Giolitti was the son of a Piedmontese magistrate and spent years as a civil servant before becoming an MP. He was an economic and political liberal and was to become the leading politician of the Liberal state. He mastered the art of *trasformismo*, which allowed him to remain in power through a variety of short-term coalitions, serving as prime minister in 1892–93, 1903–05, 1906–09, 1911–14 and 1920–21 (see Chapter 3 for more details). He died still serving as an MP in 1928, aged 86.

Glossary

Lender of last resort

The disastrous banking crisis of 1893 forced Italy to copy other advanced countries in establishing a national bank. The existence of national banks, such as the Bank of England, is a vital part of a modern and stable banking system. They can prevent private banks collapsing by lending to them and keeping them in business if they feel that the national interest justifies it. This is what is meant by 'lender of last resort'. They can also enforce regulations and sometimes mergers on banks thought to be too small or badly run.

Glossary

Trade deficit

A country has a trade deficit if the value of what it imports exceeds the value of what it exports. A prolonged trade deficit means that a country goes into debt, which can have damaging economic effects such as the currency coming under pressure. A prolonged trade deficit can often lead to the devaluation of the currency as foreign banks sell their old currency to buy currency from countries with a lower deficit. However, in the case of Italy, the influx of dollars from the USA kept the lira afloat.

Industry and agriculture

Traditional industries such as silk, cotton and wool made great strides, ceasing to be based on hand-looms and becoming mechanised. New technologies figured prominently. Camillo Olivetti began producing his famous typewriter in Piedmont in 1908 and various individuals set up motor car firms. The most famous of these was begun in 1899 in Turin by cavalry officer Giovanni Agnelli. *Fabbrica Italiana Automobili Torino* (FIAT) was to make him and his descendants a vast fortune. Others followed and Italians showed a natural talent for engineering design. In 1912, Agnelli had the foresight to move into the mass production of cheaper cars after a visit to Ford's plant in the USA.

Advert for FIAT 258, 1899

Advances were also made in agriculture. A new sugar beet industry developed with refineries springing up in the North. Wheat production increased and the use of fertiliser and scientific methods resulted in considerably higher yields. Improved transport opened up new markets within both Italy and Germany and even the USA. There were massive land reclamation and drainage schemes, although most of these were in the North. In fact the 'economic miracle' widened the North–South divide. Almost all the industrial development was in Piedmont and Lombardy. The contrast in agricultural efficiency became more stark. Wheat yields in the North were 1.5 tons per hectare compared to 0.6 in Sicily. Just before the First World War, maize yields in Lombardy were 2.5 tons per hectare compared to 0.5 in Sicily. Economic development was reinforcing the notion of two Italys: one poor and backward south of Rome, the other a modern, educated and developed Italy to the north of the capital.

Social discontent and the challenge from socialism

The rise of the working class

Take note

Make sure you understand the key words: Marxism, socialism, maximalist, anarchist and direct action. Write your own definitions of each once you have read this section, without looking back if you can.

Although Italy remained overwhelmingly agricultural, the economic developments began to create a working class of the type that existed in Britain and Germany, i.e. large numbers of workers in factories rather than day labourers or craft journeymen working in small workshops. The sugar refineries employed over 13,000 workers by 1914 and there were over 6000 workers in the new car industry in Turin. Many people from the northern countryside poured into the cities and bigger towns. Milan grew at the rate of 14,000 a year, doubling in population from 300,000 in 1880 to 600,000 by 1914. Socialist ideas spread, as did unionisation, amongst this new working class. This was clearly going to have implications for government. Such concentrated bodies of workers could be more easily mobilised for political activity and challenge to the existing authorities.

There was a long tradition in Italy of kicking against authority, even in the countryside, and there was a strong **anarchist** movement in some areas. Italian anarchists were prominent not just in assassinations in Italy, like that of King Umberto I in 1900, but also in France (President Carnot in 1894), Spain (Prime Minister Castillo in 1897) and Austria (the Empress in 1898). The anarchists might produce dramatic events but they had little long-term impact. It was essentially the policy of protest. It was an ex-anarchist, Andrea Costa, who founded the Revolutionary Socialist Party of Romagna in 1881 and became the first Socialist deputy in 1882. This party looked forward to revolution eventually but thought years of preparation would be necessary.

Marxist ideas became increasingly fashionable in the 1880s and 1890s amongst the intellectual community. One such intellectual, influenced by Marx, was the Milanese lawyer **Filippo Turati**. He was very much a member of the upper-middle class. His father was a prefect in Lombardy and his mother a devout Roman Catholic, yet he rejected their values and, after a long period of illness, embraced socialism as a new religion. Like many Italian socialists there was a moral fervour to his political beliefs and a commitment not just to redistributing wealth, but to the moral transformation of the poor into worthy citizens. Socialism saw itself as a clear rival and alternative to the Church and socialist leaders saw themselves almost as a new priesthood wrestling for the bodies (if not the souls, which they did not believe in) of the poor.

The painting *The Fourth Estate* (i.e. the 'mob' or workers), by da Volpedo in 1901, shows workers marching on strike

Glossary

Anarchists

Italian anarchists tended to be followers of the Russian revolutionany Mikhail Bakunin (1814–76). They believed all governments were repressive, even socialist ones, hence their dislike of Marxists. Their ideal society was one based on voluntary co-operation without private property. They tended to be fiercely anti-Church/religion.

Marxism

A political philosophy developed by Karl Marx (1818–83). According to Marx, all human history is driven by class conflict. In any society, the group that controls the means of production (i.e. how the wealth is produced) is the ruling class. He believed that conflict between classes over the means of production would produce a series of revolutions. First, the aristocratic landowners would be overthrown by the factory-owning classes (the bourgeoisie). A Marxist was likely to interpret the *Risorgimento* as the triumph of the bourgeoisie. Then the industrial working class (the proletariat) would overthrow the bourgeoisie and take control of the means of production. The rule of the proletariat would produce the ideal system of socialism. Among the central tenets of Marxism are a denial of religion and of a spiritual dimension; Marx was a 'materialist' who believed that there was nothing beyond the material world.

Filippo Turati

(1857–1932)

A Milanese lawyer and founder member of the Italian Workers' Party in 1892 (which became the PSI in 1893). Turati remained effective leader of the party for several years and headed the reformist wing until 1922. He also served as deputy for Milan between 1896 and 1926. He opposed Italian involvement in the First World War but called for the military defence of the nation after the defeat at Caporetto in 1917. Turati condemned the 1917 Bolshevik revolution in Russia. Expelled from the PSI in 1922, he helped to found the reformist PSU. He fled Italy in 1926 and settled in Paris, where he organised non-communist anti-fascist activity and called for socialist unity.

Working-class politics

In 1892 Turati was instrumental in bringing together a congress of socialists in Genoa. This congress adopted a programme of social reform, such as the eight-hour day, and declared the establishment of a party of the workers with the object of working towards socialism but, in the mean time, achieving social reform. This was to be achieved through parliament and therefore involved winning parliamentary seats. A group of mainly anarchist delegates to the conference refused this approach and formed a rival party devoted to revolutionary struggle. However, the leader of the Revolutionary Socialist Party, Andrea Costa, eventually threw in his lot with Turati and Turati's group rapidly emerged as the dominant left-wing party. He had succeeded in creating a major force from various squabbling groups of short-lived and ineffective parties. This of course did not prevent future splits. There remained real tension between those like Turati, who believed in reform through parliament and co-operation with bourgeois parties to bring this about, and those who favoured direct action to bring about revolution. The more extreme socialists were usually referred to as maximalists. In 1895 Turati's party renamed themselves the Italian Socialist Party (PSI). In 1900 the PSI secured 216,000 votes and 32 deputies in the Chamber.

Parallel with the emergence of a socialist party was the development of trade unions. To begin with, these were often small localised groups of workers, but in the 1890s Chambers of Labour began to grow up, linking smaller groups into bigger units, albeit on a local basis. The Chambers embraced a vague socialism and a commitment to moral improvement and social reform. They offered their members socialist baptisms and funerals and saw themselves as enemies of superstition and the Church. By 1902 there were 76 throughout the country, although they were mainly in the north. Bigger and more geographically spread trade unions on the British and German model also began to appear. These were known as Federation Unions and the most important of these was the Metal Workers Union, set up in 1901. Chambers of Labour and the Federation Unions agreed to join in an umbrella organisation – the General Confederation of Labour (CGL). Amongst the most numerous of the component unions was the *Federterra*, representing agricultural workers. By 1913, the CGL had 327,000 members. This helped to strengthen the links between the PSI and the workers as leading trade unionists tended to also be members of the PSI.

Not surprisingly, the period was marked by a wave of strikes, most of them localised. In 1901 there were 1000 strikes recorded. In 1904 a general strike was called in response to the killing of some strikers. From 1906 to 1910 there was an average of 1500 strikes a year and the inevitable violence that flared up kept alive the idea of class war and the dream of a socialist revolution. The mainly middle-class MPs, who were overwhelmingly lawyers or teachers, believed that some reform could be achieved by co-operation with liberals like Giolitti. In turn, Giolitti hoped to use concessions to buy their support in the Chamber of Deputies (the parliament of Italy). However, the largely moderate Socialist deputies (MPs) had to maintain a certain distance from the liberal governments to prove their socialist credentials to their followers, who were always likely to raise the charge of betrayal.

The extent of the Socialist challenge

The PSI steadily advanced as a political force and achieved a quarter of the votes in the 1913 elections. However, it never had more than 50,000 members, including 1300 in Milan but only 530 in Rome. In addition, there were still only 52 deputies in the Chamber – a tenth of the total – as a result of the **voting system**. Socialist candidates might secure the most votes on the first round but were pushed into second place on the second and found it hard to get a majority of the votes cast outside very militant areas. The party was also subject to bitter feuds and splits. Moderate reformers like Turati faced a constant battle with the maximalists. These extreme left-wingers were deeply suspicious of co-operation with the bourgeois parties in the Chamber and likely to denounce moderates as traitors to the working class.

In 1908, Turati and the moderates were able to defeat a group of enthusiastic revolutionaries who were expelled from the PSI and formed the **Syndicalist Party**, committed to victory through strike action. In 1912 the maximalists got their revenge and expelled some members whom they considered excessively moderate. The moderate MPs had congratulated the king on surviving an assassination attempt, conduct it was felt not worthy of true friends of the workers. They left to form a moderate reformist party. There were thus three socialist parties by 1913. Turati stayed with the PSI but was unhappy with the increasingly shrill tone of militant class warfare. Amongst the shrillest was the new editor of the party paper, *Avanti*, one **Benito Mussolini**.

Biography

Benito Mussolini

(1883–1945)

The son of a blacksmith from the Romagna, Mussolini had a violent temper and an inclination to revolutionary politics. He trained as a teacher but found his true calling as a journalist, in which profession he showed real talent. This lay in a sense of what created impact rather than in the pursuit of truth.

Mussolini founded the Italian Fascist Party in 1921 and was prime minister from 1922 to 1943. By the mid-1920s, he had created a fascist dictatorship and was known as the *Duce* (Leader). His decision to enter the Second World War in 1940 as an ally of Nazi Germany proved to be a military disaster for Italy. Mussolini was deposed in 1943 but, after being rescued by German forces, he was installed as a Nazi puppet dictator in northern Italy. In April 1945, Mussolini was captured and executed by Italian communists.

The parties of the left were always likely to fragment and thereby reduce their effectiveness. In theory the socialist groups threatened the existence of what they considered to be 'bourgeois Italy'. In reality the extremists were too small and ineffective to carry out the revolution they planned for and the moderates under Turati were prepared to work within the system. In other words, socialism could be tamed as long as circumstances did not drive the bulk of the growing working class into the arms of the extremists.

The voting system

The voting system for the Chamber of Deputies was designed to ensure that the winner had an absolute majority of the votes cast. This was achieved by a two-stage system. On the first round many groups might stand but then those securing the least votes dropped out. This therefore favoured moderates and parties of the centre.

Glossary

Syndicalist Party

Revolutionary group committed to the idea of achieving power not through the ballot box but through industrial action such as strikes. This is often referred to as direct action.

Take note

As you read through this section, try to answer these questions:
Why did the Church reject the new Italy?
Why did the Church increasingly become involved in politics from the 1890s onwards?

The papacy

(1878–1922)

Leo XIII (1878–1903) proved to be the longest living pope. He tried to heal some of the divisions caused by his predecessor and tried to reach out to the working classes.

Pius X (1903–1914) felt that some Catholic activists had become too sympathetic to socialism. He thought their influence was too great and was unhappy that they were out of the control of the church hierarchy. His response to what he described as the sin of 'modernism' was to abolish the *Opera dei Congressi* in 1904 and substitute Catholic Action, which was firmly under the control of the bishops.

Benedict XV (1914–1922) was largely concerned with the divisions within his international flock, caused by the First World War.

The Catholics

The Catholic Church saw itself as the great loser in the process of unification. The pope had lost his position as the sovereign prince of much of central Italy and Church lands had been confiscated and sold off throughout the peninsula. Pope Pius IX and his successor, **Leo XIII**, made it clear that good Catholics should also disapprove of the new Italian state and forbade them from taking part in its national elections. However, the prohibition did not apply to local elections and here Catholics began to make their power felt. The Church had founded a lay organisation for good Catholics to work through to promote moral causes and the interests of the Church. This was the *Opera dei Congressi e dei Comitati Cattolici*. It focused on education but also promoted co-operatives and rural banks to help Catholic peasants.

Two political moves by Francesco Crispi helped to increase the influence of the *Opera dei Congressi*:

- He attempted to reform charities in 1890, many of which were closely connected with the Church and Catholicism. This produced outrage.

- His reform of local government in 1893 extended the franchise, and increased Catholic influence.

Catholics increasingly came to control many local governments in the north. By 1897 the *Opera dei Congressi* controlled 3982 parish committees and 588 rural co-operative banks. It ran 24 daily newspapers and 155 journals.

The Church began to pronounce a clear message on social and economic issues. This was partly in answer to the threat of godless socialism. In 1891, the pope stressed that the Church stood for charity and class co-operation, and that it was heavily opposed to the greed of selfish capitalism. A programme was issued in Milan in 1894 and it claimed to counter the appeal of socialism with 'Christian democracy'. The programme was adopted by the *Opera dei Congressi* in 1895.

The growing influence of the Catholic Church produced a crackdown in 1897 by the government. Prefects were ordered to curb the influence of the *Opera dei Congressi*; they dissolved many of the *Opera*'s institutions and closed down Catholic papers. After 1898 the persecution was dropped and most local organisations were re-founded, but it had the effect of persuading the Church authorities to begin to co-operate with the Liberal state. Slowly, over the next few years, Catholics were allowed to take a more direct and increasing part in national politics. In 1904, **Pope Pius X** finally permitted Catholics to vote in constituencies where a socialist might win. In 1909 Catholics openly stood for election. 17 were elected, although not as representatives of the Catholic Church as such, merely as known Catholics. It was a subtle distinction.

In 1905, the *Opera dei Congressi* was reorganised and a series of unions established under the umbrella heading of Catholic Action. There were unions for youth, women, charitable causes, economic issues and to mobilise the vote. The new organisation was more firmly under the control of the bishops. There had been a feeling that the Christian democrats of the *Opera dei Congressi* were behaving a little too freely outside Church control. Under the new organisation, Catholic influence asserted itself more and more in society, particularly in the youth and women's movements. The Catholic sporting organisation FASCI also expanded rapidly, with 204 societies by 1910. A young priest from Sicily, **Father Luigi Sturzo**, was to be increasingly influential and pressed for a separate Catholic party.

The Vatican was always suspicious of Catholic accommodation with the Liberal state without the right terms for the Church. However, by 1913, the Vatican was beginning to accept Sturzo's argument that a clearly separate party was better than the kind of loose co-operation with the liberals to keep the socialists out that had been happening since 1904. In 1919 a Catholic political party was born – the Italian Popular Party (PPI) – with Sturzo as leader. The growing activity of Catholics in politics posed a real problem for the Liberal state. It made it harder for the prefects to fix elections as, like the socialists, the Church showed a real talent for mobilising the voters. The best the liberals could do was to play off the Catholics against the socialists.

The nationalist movement

A third destabilising group, threatening the nature of the Liberal state, were the nationalists, who – after the downfall of Crispi over Adowa – lacked a natural political leader. In fact, in the early years of the twentieth century, they could hardly be identified as an organised group. However, the nationalist movement developed strongly as an intellectual movement amongst the young and well-educated, particularly in the years 1909–11. A spate of journals was founded proclaiming the need for Italy to have her rightful place in the world. A **Nationalist Congress** was held in 1910 and the main journal, *L'Idea Nazionale*, was first published on 1 March 1911. Their basic platform was the demand for a more active foreign policy and greater spending on defence. It was never a mass movement like the socialists or the Catholics, both of whom proclaimed their international credentials, but it had influence in parliament and amongst the elite. Many of Italy's leading writers and poets threw their weight behind nationalism, denouncing the weakness and corruption they saw emanating from parliament and its great manipulator, Giolitti.

The bald-headed nationalist poet **Gabriele D'Annunzio** thrilled audiences with his songs and plays. The somewhat ridiculous play *The Ship*, first performed in 1908, attracted vast audiences with its bloody story of revenge and heroic deeds. It was twice filmed and even turned into an opera. Much of D'Annunzio's work was sound and fury, and perhaps signified nothing, but it excited. Many of the educated young wished to be excited. The Liberal state was not exciting.

Biography

Father Luigi Sturzo
(1871–1959)

Ordained a priest in 1894, Sturzo was something of an academic. He taught and wrote about theology and doctrine, but became increasingly interested in politics. Sturzo was one of the founder members of the PPI. He served as the party's general secretary until 1923 and, a year later, he was sent into exile because of his opposition to fascism. He returned to Italy in 1946 and became a senator in 1952.

Biography

Gabriele D'Annunzio
(1863–1938)

A prominent nationalist and major literary figure who wrote poetry and plays, D'Annunzio delighted to shock and enjoyed a reputation as a womaniser and duellist. He embraced both the extreme right and the extreme left at various times. The key idea was to be extreme.
D'Annunzio was a powerful advocate of Italian intervention in 1914–15 and volunteered to fight at the age of 52. In August 1918, as a publicity stunt, he flew over Vienna and dropped propaganda leaflets. He was appointed President of the Royal Academy of Arts by Mussolini in 1937.

Enrico Corradini addresses the First Nationalist Congress

"Just as socialism taught the proletariat the value of the class struggle, so we must teach Italy the value of the international struggle. But is not the international struggle war? Well, let there be war then! And let Nationalism arouse in Italy the will to a victorious war."

Taking it further

Try to find out more about the career of Gabriele D'Annunzio and his works. What gave him his hold on the imagination of so many of the educated young? Why was his play *The Ship* so popular?

Conclusion: How far was the Liberal state under fire?

Italy was changing rapidly in these years, particularly in the North, and this made the North–South divide even more pronounced. The growth of both socialism and political Catholicism was undermining the basis of the Liberal state and the system of *trasformismo*. Eventually it would lay the basis of the two great parties which dominated Italy after 1945: the Socialists and the Christian Democrats. In the meantime, it contributed to instability. The growth of nationalism also added to a sense that the Liberal state had failed to deliver, as multiple forces hostile to the state began to emerge. It was with all these forces that the great master of *trasformismo*, Giolitti, wrestled in the years before 1914.

Activity: Speeches

Write two short speeches by rival Socialists in 1910. One speech should be written from the point of view of a maximalist urging direct action and revolution. The other should be written from the point of view of Turati, urging the benefits of adopting the parliamentary road and co-operating with Liberals, and warning of the dangers of direct action.

Activity: Briefing

Write a brief for Crispi's successor in 1896, outlining the key issues facing Italian politics and the economy that will need to be addressed.

Activity: Radical reports

Write a newspaper article about the radicalisation of the working classes. You could do this as a socialist paper, celebrating the awakening of the workers or as a conservative paper warning of the dangers of the unruly masses.

Chapter 3 Giolitti and the response to change: Italy 1896–1914

Key questions

- What was Giolitti trying to achieve and how successful was he?
- How did Giolitti govern Italy?
- What was achieved by Giolitti?
- How did Giolitti make things worse for his successors?

Giovanni Giolitti was the great master of *trasformismo*, the greatest practitioner of politics in the Liberal state. After years learning the business of government as a civil servant in the treasury, Giolitti became an MP and learned the trade of parliamentary management. He was a thoroughgoing liberal, believing that **accommodation** and incentives were better than compulsion and, in general, political, social and economic freedom engendered human happiness. He was somewhat suspicious of the Catholic Church but not hostile and prepared to work with moderates in the clerical PPI. He had faith in the free market, but was prepared to concede social reforms to keep the socialists happy and prevent revolution. He had a rather cynical view of human nature, assuming that people pursued their self-interest first and foremost, but that, if they were able to do this, they would then be good citizens. Put crudely, he believed that everyone had their price and that most people could be reconciled to the status quo.

Timeline	
1892–93	Giolitti prime minister for the first time
1898	May riots in Milan – heavy-handed repression by the army; Luigi Pelloux appointed prime minister
1900	King Umberto I assassinated
1901	Giolitti minister of the interior
1902	Women's working day limited to 11 hours and child labour under 12 prohibited
1907	Compulsory rest day each week introduced
1911	War declared on Turkey
1912	Suffrage massively extended (first elections 1913)
1914	Red Week

Glossary

Accommodation

A political compromise achieved by taking steps towards meeting the aims and wishes of the rival party in order to win their support.

The origins of Giolitti's supremacy

Between 1896 and 1900, the Liberal state seemed so threatened on all sides that its survival was in doubt. The defeat in Abyssinia seemed to destroy the prestige of the new state and the monarchy. It brought down Crispi, the most charismatic politician that the new Italy had thrown up. His successors were driven into using excessive force to keep the system going; the stick seemed to be replacing the carrot as a means of control. In September 1897, as we have seen, the government cracked down on Catholic organisations and this harassment and persecution went on into the spring of 1898.

Take note

In what ways were the years 1896–1900 years of political crisis? Make a list of these crises and note down three facts or examples about each one.

Year	Prime Minister	Politics
1896–98	Antonio Starabba	Right
1898–1900	Luigi Pelloux	Right
1900–01	Giuseppe Saracco	Left
1901–03	Giuseppe Zanardelli	Left
1903–05	Giovanni Giolitti	Left
1905	Tommaso Tittoni	Right
1905–06	Alessandro Fortis	Left
1906	Sidney Sonnino	Right
1906–09	Giovanni Giolitti	Left
1909–10	Sidney Sonnino	Right
1910–11	Luigi Luzzati	Right
1911–14	Giovanni Giolitti	Left

Prime ministers of Italy, 1896–1914

Even more dramatic was the repression of a series of violent riots in Milan by the army. A bad harvest in 1897 had produced a 50% increase in the price of wheat and bread. There were demonstrations and riots throughout the country in early 1898. Nervous policemen shot rioters and in Milan a full-scale insurrection broke out in May. The police lost control of the situation and military units under General Bava Beccaris were called in to restore order, killing 118 and wounding 450 according to the official figures. Socialist and Catholic activists were arrested and sentenced to long periods of imprisonment. Turati of the PSI was given 12 years.

King Umberto I inflamed the situation more by decorating Beccaris with one of the highest military honours – the Cross of Savoy. He then appointed another general, Luigi Pelloux, as prime minister. There was talk of pushing through various repressive measures limiting freedom and in effect undermining the liberal constitution. Failing to get these through parliament, there was an attempt to push them through by royal decree, but this broke down as the courts pronounced them invalid. There was physical fighting in the Chamber of Deputies itself and the whole system seemed to be self-destructing. General Pelloux called an election which produced strong gains for the Left, including Socialists, radical liberals and those constitutional liberals opposed to the repressive measures. Pelloux resigned and, as a final dramatic climax to the crisis, the king himself was assassinated by an anarchist in July. The new king, **Victor Emmanuel III**, was prepared to adopt a more conciliatory approach. There would be a return to the carrot rather than the stick and the man to feed carrots to the stubborn Italian donkey was Giovanni Giolitti.

Biography

Victor Emmanuel III

1869–1947

Victor Emmanuel inherited the throne at the age of 30. He was rather shy, short and, like most of the House of Savoy, devoted to the army. Despite being rather uncharismatic, he was anxious to be a good constitutional monarch. His father had informed him that all he needed to do to be king was 'to be able to ride a horse, sign his name and read a newspaper'. He managed all three tasks but found Mussolini's new march modelled on the German goosestep too difficult because of his little legs.

Victor Emmanuel III in 1915

Giolitti

Giolitti was at the centre of government for so long that he thoroughly mastered the dark arts of manipulation to achieve majorities in parliament. He did not necessarily approve of such methods, but accepted them as inevitable. He had no love for southern landlords, but they were a key element in ensuring government majorities by rigging the vote throughout the South. 103 out of 137 MPs from the South supported the government in 1904. He was prepared to bargain with Catholics and formed secret electoral pacts to keep out hostile socialists. He also tried to win over moderate socialists and offered Turati a cabinet post in 1904 and again in 1911.

Giolitti could be tough if he had to be, as when he ordered prefects to suspend councils. This happened in 1904 when voters elected a Catholic council in Bassano. But in general he preferred concession and accommodation. His power was indeed enormous, and as he had held power for so long he had appointed a large proportion of all the key office holders such as the prefects and members of the upper house, the Senate. Hundreds of powerful men were grateful to him and were in his debt.

Giolitti also mastered the technique of resigning at the opportune moment and not appearing to have too much power, letting others front for him for a time. In 1901, he was appointed minister of the interior and, although he was still the real master of the government, he allowed another the prestige of the top job. He took over as prime minister in November 1903 and held the position until March 1905. Faced with a threatening rail strike, he resigned and let his successor deal with the strike, then returned a year later and served until December 1909. After another opportune break, he returned in March 1911 and served until March 1914.

Giolitti (right) walking with Victor Emmanuel and his wife, 1904

Giolitti's achievements and difficulties

Giolitti's achievements were many, not least holding the fractious Italian people together with minimal violence. It was a period of real economic progress and Giolitti deserves some of the credit (see Chapter 2). Balanced budgets led to judicious government spending to stimulate the economy and alleviate suffering, such as when the horrific earthquake of 1908 devastated Messina in Sicily and killed up to 100,000 people. Even before this tragedy, spending on public works rose by 50% between 1900 and 1907. The rolling stock of the nationalised railways was much improved. Roads, aqueducts and irrigation schemes were launched in the South. It was a sign of the success of these measures that, instead of moving to the cities, peasants left their hovels in hilltop towns and settled once more on isolated farms or in hamlets. Greater security as well as better facilities made this possible.

There were a series of reforms to win over, or at least pacify, the working class.

- Child labour was prohibited and women limited to 11 working hours a day.

- Night work in bakeries was prohibited.

- National insurance provision for sickness and old age was extended and a compulsory weekly rest day was introduced in 1907.

- A Maternity Fund for all female industrial workers was established in 1910. 40 lire was provided at each birth, jointly provided by the state, the employer and employee contributions.

Giolitti's greatest concession to the Socialists and their working-class supporters was the strict neutrality he insisted that the state maintain in industrial disputes. He made it plain in a **letter of 1906** to the police and prefects that they were not to take the employers' part in strikes.

Giolitti in a letter dated 1906

"I remind all State officials that in this period of profound social transformation government action must be inspired both by absolute neutrality in the struggles between capital and labour and by affectionate concern for the legitimate aspirations of the working classes."

Biography

Count Otterino Gentiloni

(1865–1916)

A leading lay member of Catholic Action, which was established in 1905. Gentiloni was appointed by Pope Pius X to head the political wing of Catholic Action, dealing with electoral matters. He was viewed as safely conservative and opposed to the 'modernist' wing of Catholic reformers who shared many of the socialists' aspirations. His secret deal with Giolitti in 1912 was vital in enabling Giolitti to survive the 1913 elections, which had a much enlarged electorate. The Pact or *il Patto Gentiloni* reduced the potential challenge from the socialists.

Take note

As you read through this section, consider: What developments were undermining the political system of which Giolitti was the master? Why did Giolitti fall from power in 1914?

Partly as a result of the torrent of strikes, real wages in both agriculture and industry went up by 2.5% per annum between 1901 and 1911. This amounted to a real improvement in the standard of living and the daily calorie intake improved significantly. However, Giolitti's policy of neutrality was not popular with some employers who felt that workers were getting out of hand.

Perhaps his most important reform, and certainly the riskiest, was the decision to extend the franchise massively in 1912. Giolitti felt that only by bringing the masses into the political process was it possible to end their alienation from it. The war with Turkey over Libya in 1911–12 (see below) was used to justify the extension of the franchise; it was impossible to ask men to fight and then deny them political rights. The electorate rose from under 3 million to 8.5 million. All literate men over 21 were enfranchised and all men over 30 whether literate or not. Large numbers of illiterates – and in the South illiteracy rates were as high as 70% in 1912 – now had the vote. It did not produce a massive immediate change, although the Socialist vote went up to 22.8% from 19%. However, it did weaken the hold of the municipal elites on elections and, in the long-term, it weakened the traditional methods of election control by the prefects. Even in 1913, Giolitti had to rely heavily on a secret deal with the Election Union of Catholic Action under **Count Gentiloni**. Gentiloni later claimed that 228 liberals who backed Giolitti were dependent on Catholic support. It was a sign that the old system would not last in an age of real democracy.

The decline and fall of Giolitti

The tragedy of Giolitti was that he lived in an age of lunatic idealism. On the Left, figures like the young Mussolini burned with ardour to bring down the system in violent revolution. Like many on the extremes, Mussolini was much influenced by **Georges Sorel**'s *Reflections on Violence*, published in 1908. This book suggested that human beings were driven not by reason but by passion, and that the romance of violence could motivate people to make change. The syndicalists were even more enthralled than Mussolini by this idea. On the Right, the likes of D'Annunzio (when he was not engaged in torrid love affairs or fighting duels) were urging a cleansing of Italy by blood. It seemed that, in some ways, Giolitti was a lone 'grown up' in a hormonal teenage Italy.

Giolitti was much criticised for his unassertive foreign policy. When taken to task for appointing a political nobody as foreign secretary, he had replied 'But he is only foreign secretary'. Defence spending had been held down and no attempt had been made to repeat Crispi's bid for a great navy. The growing nationalist movement after 1909 was partly a response to this indifference of the government to Italy's international position. Many rich landowners and businessmen were alienated by what they felt was a pro-union government, and gave funding to the nationalists.

Giolitti decided in 1911 that a short little war for control of Libya could be risked to take the wind out of the nationalists' sails. Italy had long held ambitions to build an empire on the southern shores of the Mediterranean.

France had grabbed Tunis in 1881, much to Italy's horror, and Britain had taken control of Egypt the following year. Only Libya remained under the nominal rule of Turkey. Turkish power seemed to be on the point of extinction and the fear was that, if Italy did not act, France would add Libya to her extensive North African empire, rubbing salt into Italy's wounds over Tunis. Italy declared war on Turkey and invaded Libya in September. The war proved much harder to win than Giolitti anticipated. He was helped by the assault on Turkey by various Balkan nations in 1912 but, even when Turkey made peace and transferred Libya to Italy, the local Arab population had to be brought under control. This was no easy task and the conflict was extremely brutal. Atrocities were widespread. Captured Italian troops were often nailed to palm trees with their eyes sewn up and their genitals removed. Thousands of Libyans were hanged. Possibly an eighth of the entire Libyan population were to die before Italian authority became effective.

Italian soldiers escort Arab prisoners in Libya, November 1911

The war did not prove to be the good move Giolitti anticipated. He was blamed for the slowness and the cost of the conquest and the nationalists got the credit for the victory. The socialists opposed the war, causing division between them and Giolitti. Within the Socialist Party, the extremists (the maximalists) had gained control in 1912, marginalising Turati and those who wished to co-operate with Giolitti. His secret deal with the Catholics in the election of 1913 upset the radical liberals, who were bitterly anti-clerical. Slowly his majority seeped away and, in March 1914, he resigned and the king appointed the more right-wing **Antonio Salandra**. Salandra was more acceptable to nationalist opinion and, against Giolitti's wishes, he was to take Italy into the European war which broke out in August 1914.

Biography

Georges Sorel

1847–1922

Sorel was a French engineer but turned to writing on politics and revolutionary theory in his retirement. He stressed the power of the irrational in motivating human beings. Myth was often more important than reason and reality. His most important book was *Reflections on Violence*, published in book form in 1908. The book suggested that violent acts of revolution could effectively transform society. Mussolini was much influenced by Sorel's ideas.

Biography

Antonio Salandra

(1853–1931)

A prominent moderate liberal and former university professor, Salandra served as prime minister from 1914 to 1916 but failed to impose political control over the Italian military campaign. After the war, he backed fascist policies and was made a senator by Mussolini in 1928.

Taking it further

Try to find out more about the horrific earthquake in Sicily and Calabria in 1908 and the government's response.

Why was it so devastating? What did the government do to help those affected?

Conclusion: Giolitti – a success or a failure?

The years 1896–1900 had been years of political crisis, marked by strikes, violent riots and an attempt, backed by the king, to change the constitution in a more authoritarian direction. The attempt failed and in 1900 the king was assassinated. His successor, Victor Emmanuel III, was more inclined to try to make the existing system work. The key figure in doing this was Giolitti.

Giolitti sought to tame the growing working class by concessions and to avoid confrontation with the Church. He hoped to produce a stable, prosperous Italy. His achievements were considerable, despite continuing strikes. He delivered a series of social reforms, and living standards and real wages rose. Socialist moderates like Turati worked with him but, despite his own inclination to accept Giolitti's offer of a government position, co-operation had to be at arm's length for fear of arousing the suspicions of the more extreme members of the Socialist Party. These maximalists and the revolutionary groups outside the PSI, such as the Syndicalists and anarchists, kept up the chant for revolution. However, the threat of revolution was not realistic and the extremists were simply a small but noisy minority. Giolitti was slowly taming the working classes and their more sensible leaders.

A similar situation existed with regard to the Catholic Church. In theory there was no dialogue between Giolitti and the Church, and the Vatican continued to deny official recognition to the Italian state. Once again, reality was at odds with appearance. The Church entered into secret negotiations and deals which indicated that, in time, full reconciliation would take place. Perhaps Giolitti's most serious failure lay in the growing nationalist movement, whose very growth was a commentary on his unassertive foreign policy. In typical fashion, he tried to appease them with a little war and the conquest of Libya. The attempt backfired, and helped to precipitate his downfall. Overall, he was a remarkably successful politician, handling a series of difficult issues with skill. The fact that he did not manage to solve all of Italy's problems is not the point – politicians never can. He gave Italy nearly 14 years of growing prosperity and stability. Given what had gone before and what was to come, this was no mean achievement.

Activity: Political debate

1   Write a 100-word speech by D'Annunzio violently denouncing Giolitti (see Chapter 2 for the nationalist perspective).

2   Write another 100-word speech by a revolutionary socialist denouncing Giolitti (see Chapter 2 for the revolutionary socialist perspective).

3   Write a riposte by Giolitti to the critical speeches above, defending his policies.

Skills Builder 1: **Writing in paragraphs**

In the examination you will have to write an essay-style answer on this topic, in approximately 40 minutes. When producing an essay-style answer, it is important that you write in paragraphs. You will need to make a number of points to build up your argument so that it answers the question you have been asked. You should write a paragraph to address each point.

What should you include in a paragraph?

In a paragraph you should:

- make a point to support your argument and answer the question
- provide evidence to support your point
- explain how your evidence supports your point
- explain how your points relate to the essay question.

Remember: POINT — EVIDENCE — EXPLANATION

It is important that you construct your answer this way. If you just 'tell a story' in which you produce factual knowledge without explanation in relation to the question, you will not get high marks.

An example

Here is an example of a question asking you to produce not a story, but an explanation:

> (A) Why did the Italian economy develop and grow so rapidly in the years 1896–1914?

The information to answer this question can be found in Section 1. The reasons you could include are:

- government policies
- new technology – hydroelectric power
- a reformed banking sector
- remittances from the USA.

As you plan, it is important to have a clear idea about the significance of these reasons. To do this, you must decide which factor was the most important. Your answer should convince the examiner that your opinion is correct.

Here is an example of a paragraph which could form part of your answer:

The development of hydroelectric power, which could be transported and which – with its alpine rivers – Italy could easily generate, transformed Italy's industrial growth. Italy had been held back by an absence of coal, a key basis of energy in nineteenth-century technology. This alone would have had limited impact, although generation grew from 50,000 KW to 1 million KW by 1914. Its importance was that it enabled other key industries to grow, such as the steel plants of Terni, which fuelled naval and rail expansion.

This is a good paragraph because:

- it begins with a clear statement which assesses a reason for growth
- it comments that this has to be *related* to other reasons thereby recognising the complexity of the explanation
- the opening statement is backed up by evidence. It provides details of growth and quantifies it.

Activity: Spot the mistake

Below are three paragraphs which attempt to explain why the Italian economy grew between 1896 and 1914. However, although the information in each paragraph is correct, there are mistakes in the way each paragraph is written. Your task is to spot the mistake in each paragraph and write one sentence of advice to the author of each paragraph explaining how they could do better.

Example 1

Many industries grew in these years, the most dramatic being the car industry. FIAT was established in 1899 in Turin and in 1912 Agnelli, the founder, adopted American mass-production techniques. By 1914 there were 6000 workers producing cars in Italy. Likewise, an electrical industry developed in these years and Olivetti began manufacturing typewriters. In all these ways it seemed that Italy was at the forefront of technology.

Example 2

Hydroelectric power could be generated by the fast-flowing rivers of the alpine regions of Italy in Piedmont, Lombardy and the Veneto. There was a key technological breakthrough that allowed such energy to be transported and generation grew rapidly. Coal still continued to be imported and imports grew rapidly from 4 million tons a year to 11 million tons.

Example 3

There were many reasons for the rapid economic development. The development of hydroelectric power and a crucial reform of the banking system greatly assisted the development of many industries such as the vast steel works of Terni, which became the biggest hydroelectric-powered plant on Earth. The South remained very backward and did not really share in the rapid development of the North.

Answers

Example 1 – this paragraph tells the story of some important developments but does not really offer an explanation.

Example 2 – this paragraph contains lots of detailed information, some of which could be related to the question but in this form is not.

Example 3 – this paragraph is generally well written, but the final sentence goes off the point of the question.

Activity: Write your own paragraph

Now try writing a paragraph on one of the other reasons for Italy's economic development. The information you require is found throughout Section 1.

Remember to begin your paragraph by stating which factor you are going to address. Make sure that you support your answer with factual knowledge and evidence. Then conclude your paragraph by explaining how the evidence it provides answers the question.

You may find the following steps a useful guide:
1. First decide what point you are going to make. Make sure that the point is relevant to the question you have been asked, for example: government policy.
2. Decide which evidence you will use to support your point. But choose carefully – make sure that it is relevant and is linked directly to the point you are making.
3. Write your paragraph by:

- presenting your point
- backing your point up with evidence
- explaining how the evidence supports your point
- explaining how your point relates to the essay question.

Remember: POINT — EVIDENCE — EXPLANATION

Extension work

Here is an example of the style of question often used in the examination. It asks you to make a judgment about causes:

> (B) How far was Italy's economic weakness responsible for her lack of international importance in the years 1896–1914?

If you were writing an essay-style answer to this question, you would be expected to select information which helps explain why Italy was regarded as the least of the great powers in these years. Clearly, the stated factor of Italy's economic state and ranking will need attention and then other factors such as the lack of importance accorded to foreign policy by Giolitti, the low defence spending, the internal divisions and the complex relations with other key powers such as France, Austria, Germany and Britain. You may also wish to add factors of your own. Using the steps outlined above to help you, write a paragraph to form part of an essay in answer to the question.

Chapter 4 Italy and the First World War

Key questions

- Why did Italy decide to remain neutral in 1914?
- Why did entry into the First World War cause divisions within Italy?
- What impact did the war have on the Italian economy?

On 28 June 1914, Archduke Franz Ferdinand, heir to the Austro-Hungarian throne, and his wife were assassinated in Sarajevo by Bosnian Serbs. Within six weeks, their deaths had triggered the First World War. Italy initially remained neutral but eventually entered the war on the side of the Entente Powers, later known as the Allies, in May 1915, hoping for significant territorial rewards. Involvement in the conflict, however, proved to be deeply damaging. The war hardened the pre-1914 divisions within Italy, placed the economy under great strain and exposed the weaknesses of the Italian army. Criticism of the liberal political system mounted during these years and sharp differences between **neutralists** and **interventionists** emerged. Italy could claim victory in 1918 but, in reality, it had had a disappointing and divisive war.

Timeline

March 1914	Antonio Salandra formed a new government
August 1914	First World War began; Italy declared its neutrality and negotiated with both sides
November 1914	Benito Mussolini expelled from the Socialist Party after calling for Italian intervention in the war
April 1915	Italy signed the Treaty of London with the Entente Powers
May 1915	Intervention crisis; Italy declared war on Austria-Hungary
August 1916	Italian army captured Gorizia; Italy declared war on Germany
October 1917	Italian defeat at Caporetto; Vittorio Orlando formed a new government
October 1918	Italian victory at Vittorio Veneto
November 1918	First World War ended with Italy on the winning side

From neutrality to intervention, August 1914–May 1915

Italy stays neutral

Unlike the **Central Powers** and the **Entente Powers**, Italy did not enter the First World War in August 1914. Instead, it declared its neutrality. Although Italy was still formally part of the Triple Alliance, Austria-Hungary declared war on Serbia in late July without consulting its southern ally in advance. This meant that Italy was under no formal obligation to offer support. The Italian government also wanted to preserve friendly relations with Britain, not least because the latter supplied most of Italy's coal and possessed a powerful navy. The population as a whole – including most Catholics and socialists – appeared to favour neutrality. Giolitti and a majority of deputies in the Chamber endorsed the public mood. They were convinced that, after the recent invasion of Libya in 1911, Italy lacked the economic strength required for a major war. Instead, Giolitti suggested, the nation could gain 'a great deal' by bargaining with both sides to stay out of the war.

Neutralists and interventionists

Italian politicians were divided over whether to remain neutral (neutralist) or to become involved (intervene – interventionist) in the war. Neutralists feared that Italy was not ready for war, or that the war would harm the country and the economy; interventionists feared what would happen if they were not on the winning side at the war's end.

The Central and Entente Powers

The Central Powers (Germany and Austria-Hungary) went to war against the Entente Powers (Britain, France and Russia) in 1914. Italy had joined the Central Powers in the Triple Alliance in 1882 but sided with the Entente in April 1915.

Take note

As you read through this section, consider why Italy remained neutral in August 1914 and then entered the First World War in May 1915. Make a list of the key factors influencing each decision. Was public opinion important in either case? As you read through the next section, identify the main reasons for Italy's poor military performance between May 1915 and October 1917. How far did problems on the home front contribute to the Italian army's problems?

Glossary

Sacred egoism

A phrase used by Salandra which indicated that he would negotiate with the other powers purely to secure gains for Italy.

Futurism

A strongly nationalistic and imperialistic cultural movement of the early twentieth century, futurism valued action, speed and violence. It also embraced the virtues of modern technology. Filippo Marinetti, a writer, was the most famous futurist.

Syndicalism

A radical form of socialism which argued that the trade unions would overthrow the capitalist system through strike action and then become the key political and economic organisations of the new society.

Even so, the policy of neutrality posed a number of problems. If the Entente Powers were victorious, they would have little incentive to hand over the Austrian land Italy wanted (Trentino and Trieste); further, Russia would become a major rival in the Balkans and the Adriatic. If the Central Powers won the war, they might seek to punish Italy for its 'betrayal' of the Triple Alliance. Consequently, Prime Minister Antonio Salandra and Foreign Minister Sidney Sonnino held secret negotiations with both sides to see what price Italy could secure for its active support.

Salandra's approach to these talks was one of '**sacred egoism**' and, in September 1914, he remarked that 'if I thought I had had the opportunity to restore Trentino and Trieste to Italy and that I had let it slip, I would not have a moment's peace for the rest of my life'. He also concluded that the Italian monarchy and other national institutions would not survive a peace treaty which did not give Italy political and territorial rewards.

The intervention crisis, May 1915

Ultimately, Britain and France made the most attractive offer. On 26 April 1915, Italy agreed to enter the war on the side of the Entente by signing the Treaty of London. In return, Italy was to receive the South Tyrol, Trentino, Istria, Trieste and much of Dalmatia. Just two men – Salandra and Sonnino – committed Italy to this course of action. The king's endorsement was required in the final weeks leading up to the agreement but both parliament and the public were kept completely in the dark. By this stage, though, a sizeable minority of Italians, including nationalists, **futurists**, **syndicalists** and dissident socialists, were pro-war.

One of the most prominent interventionists was Benito Mussolini (see page 19), a revolutionary socialist who edited the left-wing daily newspaper *Avanti!* ('Forward!'). In October 1914, Mussolini publicly criticised outright neutrality and resigned from the newspaper. A month later, after calling for Italy to enter the war as an ally of the Entente, he was expelled from the Socialist Party.

The decision for war was driven by domestic political considerations as well. Salandra hoped that a successful military campaign would consolidate his position as national leader and enable him to outmanoeuvre his rival, Giolitti. Yet, when rumours of an agreement began to circulate in early May, more than 300 deputies left their visiting cards at the hotel in Rome where Giolitti was staying to show their continued support for neutrality. Without a parliamentary majority for intervention, Salandra resigned on 13 May 1915.

Giolitti was asked to form a new government but soon gave up once it became clear that Italy would be humiliated if it now rejected the Treaty of London, having already abandoned the Triple Alliance. He also feared that the king, who had sent telegrams endorsing the agreement with Britain and France, might be forced to abdicate.

At the same time, interventionist demonstrations took place in major cities. Gabriele D'Annunzio delivered inflammatory pro-war speeches to large audiences in Rome and Mussolini attracted a crowd of 30,000 in Milan. These gatherings called for Italy's immediate entry into the conflict, denounced Giolitti and the neutralists as traitors, and condemned the parliamentary system for 'betraying' the *Risorgimento*.

On 16 May, the king reinstated Salandra as prime minister. Giolitti accepted defeat and left the capital. Four days later, the Chamber shifted its position: it granted the government full emergency powers and economic resources by a majority of 407 to 74. The Socialist Party, unlike its Western European counterparts, voted against and remained opposed to war. Then, on 24 May, Italy declared war on Austria-Hungary. Salandra called on the nation to put 'internal discords' aside and come together in 'marvellous moral unity' to secure victory and complete the work of the *Risorgimento*. Italy did not declare war on Germany until 28 August 1916.

The manner in which Italy entered the First World War fostered a myth of 'interventionism' which proved to be damaging and divisive. According to this myth, a handful of senior politicians, driven on by a vocal pro-war minority, had committed the nation to the conflict despite opposition from parliament and the dominant forces in Italian government. In fact, Italy joined the European war in the traditional diplomatic way (with the prime minister, foreign minister and king making policy) and for the usual reason – the promise of rewards. Parliament, although overwhelmingly in favour of neutrality, accepted the decision for war. Furthermore, the interventionist groups exerted little real influence over the events of May 1915. Nonetheless, the myth had two disastrous consequences for Italy:

- It helped to harden the attitudes of many interventionists against parliament and the 'unpatriotic', and strengthen their demands for more territory.

- More importantly, it exaggerated the significance of individuals such as D'Annunzio and Mussolini in the intervention crisis and allowed them to claim the credit for Italy's entry into the war.

Italy's war, May 1915–November 1918

Military stalemate: 1915–1916

Salandra's government planned a rapid military strike to make territorial gains but the Italian forces were not up to the task. Hindered by inadequate equipment, poor leadership and disease, the **Italian army** suffered a total of 246,000 casualties on the Austrian front (see map below) in the second half of 1915. The hoped-for quick victory did not materialise and the fighting in the alpine region became an inconclusive and drawn-out affair. During the first two years, the Italian army had only one real success: the capture of **Gorizia** in August 1916.

Italian army

During the war, nearly five million Italian men were conscripted and the allocation of duties sharpened North–South and peasant-worker tensions. Most front-line soldiers were southern peasants and agricultural workers. Skilled northern workers were sent instead to 'safer' army engineering or artillery units or else assigned to armament factories away from the combat zone. Soldiers were badly paid (half a lira per day), poorly fed, subjected to harsh military discipline and entitled to just one 15-day period of leave each year. These conditions led to low morale – 55,000 deserted between early 1917 and early 1918.

Biography

Paolo Boselli

(1838–1932)

Like his predecessor, Boselli was a moderate liberal ex-university professor. He led a 'national unity' coalition government. Boselli exerted little political control over Italian military strategy and resigned after the defeat at Caporetto.

The Battle of Gorizia (August 1916)

Known also as the Sixth Battle of the Isonzo, this was by far the most successful of the 11 attacks initiated by the Italian army along the Isonzo river. The offensive was launched on 6 August and, three days later, the town of Gorizia was captured by the Italian forces, who also established a bridgehead over the Isonzo. General Luigi Cadorna, the Italian chief of staff, was well satisfied and halted the attack on 17 August. Although the offensive resulted in 51,000 Italian and 41,000 Austro-Hungarian casualties, the Battle of Gorizia raised Italian morale and encouraged Italy's government to declare war on Germany on 28 August 1916.

Biography

General Luigi Cadorna

(1850–1928)

As the Italian chief of staff from 1914 to 1917, Cadorna fiercely opposed any political interference in military affairs and ordered numerous largely unsuccessful infantry attacks against the Austrian forces. He was a rigid disciplinarian, authorising the execution of over 750 Italian soldiers and sacking 217 officers for 'incompetence'. Cadorna was dismissed after the Caporetto defeat.

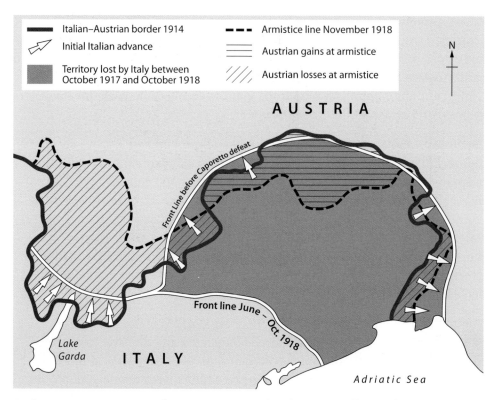

—— Italian–Austrian border 1914	- - - Armistice line November 1918
Initial Italian advance	Austrian gains at armistice
Territory lost by Italy between October 1917 and October 1918	Austrian losses at armistice

By late summer 1917, Italy's war appeared to be unravelling. The Russian army was disintegrating, American military intervention had yet to have an impact and, within the Italian ranks, morale was low. At home, public confidence in the war effort was fragile. **Paolo Boselli**'s government, which had replaced Salandra's administration in June 1916, lacked energy. Vittorio Orlando, the interior minister, was widely criticised by interventionists as 'soft' on defeatism. The Socialist Party remained opposed to the conflict and neutralist deputies still held a majority in parliament.

Two events in August 1917 further soured the popular mood. Pope Benedict XV made a public appeal for the warring nations to stop 'the useless slaughter' which had a marked effect on Italian morale. Shortly afterwards, bread riots broke out in Turin, Italy's chief armaments centre.

Disaster at Caporetto, October 1917

Worse was to come. On 24 October 1917, Austro-Hungarian forces, strengthened by seven German divisions, broke through the Italian lines at Caporetto and pushed down to the River Piave (25 miles inside Italy), which became the new war zone. Hundreds of thousands of Italian soldiers fled in confusion. Caporetto was a national humiliation and a turning point in Italy's war effort. Within a few days, Italy suffered huge military losses (40,000 casualties, 280,000 prisoners of war and 350,000 deserters) and relinquished its wartime territorial gains and a large part of the Veneto too. It then had to fight the Central Powers inside its own borders. **General Luigi Cadorna**, the Italian chief of staff, refused to accept responsibility, blaming instead the pope, Giolitti, the neutralist left-wingers and his own troops, who 'cravenly withdrew'. The Boselli government, however, resigned on 25 October.

A group of Italian soldiers on a mountain trail with their bicycles, c.1916

Biography

Vittorio Orlando
(1860–1952)

A professor of law, Orlando served in the Boselli government as interior minister before serving as prime minister from 1917 to 1919. He was a strong supporter of Italy's participation in the war. His political position was undermined by his apparent failure to secure Italian interests at the Paris Peace Conference of 1919 (see page 39).

General Armando Diaz
(1861–1928)

Diaz joined the army in 1881 and proved himself a capable field commander. He became a member of the General Staff in 1914 and was one of the more successful generals during the Isonzo offensives. After the Italian defeat at Caporetto, Diaz replaced Cadorna as chief of staff. He was able to stabilise the Piave front and partially rebuild the morale of the Italian army. With British and French assistance, Diaz repelled a Central Powers' offensive there on June 1918 and then brought about the collapse of the Austrian forces at the Battle of Vittorio Veneto. After the war, Diaz was ennobled and given the informal title 'Duke of Victory'. He served as minister of war (1922–24) under Mussolini but then retired due to poor health.

Caporetto created a wave of nationalism which had not previously existed in wartime Italy. Until then, most Italians had reluctantly accepted involvement in a conflict fought at the border but now the country had been invaded by the Central Powers. In December 1917, more than 150 deputies and 90 senators established the Parliamentary Union for National Defence. Local vigilante bodies were also formed to dispense crude street justice to the 'unpatriotic'. Many members of these grass-roots nationalist groups became supporters of fascism after the war.

A victory of sorts, October–November 1918

After Caporetto, the new prime minister, **Vittorio Orlando**, removed Cadorna and the Italian army regrouped under his successor, **General Armando Diaz**. With the help of six French and British divisions, the Italians repelled a massive Central Powers assault on the Piave front in June 1918. Four months later, the Austrian military effort collapsed. On 25 October, Italian forces, again with British and French support, launched an offensive over the Piave and by 29 October had taken the strategic town of Vittorio Veneto. The Austrians retreated in disorder back across the border. On 3 November, Italian troops captured Trentino and entered Trieste. At Austria's request, an armistice was signed the next day and Germany stopped fighting a week later. Caporetto had been avenged and Italy emerged as one of the victorious nations, but at a heavy cost: 600,000 Italian soldiers had been killed in the conflict.

The Italian war economy

The 'industrial mobilisation' system

In 1915, many feared the Italian economy would be unable to cope with the demands imposed by a drawn-out conflict. Indeed, the war brought severe financial pressures and led to serious social discontent. In August 1917, for example, bread shortages sparked a full-scale riot in Turin which claimed some 50 lives. Nevertheless, although there were persistent shortages of vital raw materials, such as coal and steel, Italy performed something of an 'economic miracle' when it came to the war effort.

Biography

General Alfredo Dallolio

(1853–1952)

An artillery officer, Dallolio was appointed under-secretary of state for munitions in July 1915. He was responsible for weapons production and the smooth running of the Italian war economy. Widely regarded as a success, Dallolio enlisted the support of key industrialists and placed some 2000 factories under military control. Nevertheless, despite his efforts, equipment shortages continued to affect the army, partly because Italy relied heavily on imported fuel and raw materials. The defeat at Caporetto weakened his position and he eventually resigned in May 1918, following a series of financial scandals. Dallolio served Mussolini in the same role between 1935 and 1939.

Take note

As you read through this section, identify the strengths and weaknesses of the 'industrial mobilisation' system and the main economic problems caused by the war. What condition was the Italian economy in by November 1918?

The army possessed just 613 machine guns in 1915 but, three years later, the total had risen to nearly 20,000. By then, the military also had over 7000 artillery pieces in operation – more than the British. Between 1914 and 1918, annual vehicle production at FIAT increased from 4500 to 25,000, making the company Europe's leading truck and lorry manufacturer. Furthermore, an aeronautical industry sprang up virtually from scratch and, in 1918 alone, 6500 planes were built.

The driving force behind the Italian war effort was the **industrial mobilisation system** of economic planning. To raise production, the government established an Under-Secretariat (later Ministry) of Arms and Munitions which was headed by **General Alfredo Dallolio**. Dallolio proved to be a dynamic organiser who ensured that, through his department, the state offered cheap loans, payment in advance and attractive contracts to favoured firms and industrialists. Companies central to the war effort (and there were 1976 of them by November 1918) were placed under industrial mobilisation, which regulated hours of work and wages, prohibited strikes and subjected employees to military discipline.

Some 905,000 workers were organised in this way. Of these, over one-third (331,000) were men excused from military service. Women accounted for about a quarter of the armament labour force and the rest were recruited mainly from the peasantry. Most industrial workers resented this military-style supervision, partly because of the long hours. By 1916, a 75-hour week was the norm at FIAT. A 25% fall in real wages during the war merely sharpened this sense of grievance. Frontline soldiers and interventionists, however, regarded urban workers, with their secure jobs away from the fighting, as spineless shirkers. This perception was to provide a potent source of division and bitterness in post-war Italy.

Only a handful of companies in the 'industrial mobilisation' programme, such as FIAT (motor vehicles), Breda (engineering), Ansaldo and Ilva (steel), and Montecatini (chemicals), really benefited from the war. These firms expanded rapidly, made huge profits and absorbed many of their competitors. FIAT's workforce rose dramatically from 6000 to 30,000 and its capital increased from 25 million to 125 million lire. Ansaldo and Ilva bought up iron mines, engineering plants and shipping lines. Towards the end of the war, these industrial giants were also competing with each other to buy leading Italian banks in order to guarantee themselves credit and deny it to their rivals. Both the workers and soldiers denounced these companies as 'sharks' and war profiteers.

The cost of the war

Most of this economic growth, of course, had been generated by massive state spending on war-related items. Consequently, the major firms faced the prospect of severe contraction when peacetime conditions returned and government orders dried up. The total sum paid out by the state during the conflict was around 41 billion lire (at pre-war prices) and, by the end of the war, Italy faced a serious budget deficit of 23.3 billion lire.

To help finance the war effort, the authorities took out foreign loans from Britain and the USA which contributed to a five-fold increase in the national debt between 1914 and 1919. The government also printed more money to cover its wartime spending but this resulted in **inflationary price rises**.

The war deepened the North–South divide too. The war boom of 1915–18 mainly benefited north-west Italy, where most of the arms firms were located. Industrial centres in this region, such as Milan and Turin, experienced population growth of over 20% in the decade after 1911. These developments strengthened the perception that there were 'two nations' – a relatively affluent industrialised urban North and an economically backward, rural South. More than 2.5 million peasants and labourers from the countryside served in the army between 1915 and 1918, leaving older men, women and youths to tend the crops. Nonetheless, food production was maintained at about 95% of the pre-war level. This feat clearly revealed the extent of rural overpopulation and the size of the surplus agricultural labour force. Government propaganda, and official measures promoting **agricultural co-operatives** on uncultivated land, raised peasant expectations that smallholdings would be widely available after the war. During 1918, landowners became increasingly concerned as peasants vented their frustration by organising unofficial land occupations in the regions of Latium and Emilia. It seemed certain that, once the rural troops had returned to their villages, the peasant clamour for land would intensify.

Conclusion: Did the war unite Italians?

In some ways, the First World War fostered a sense of Italian nationalism through shared domestic and military experience of the conflict. The defeat at Caporetto – and subsequent invasion – certainly galvanised Italian patriotism. Having said this, the war did more to divide Italians. By November 1918, the nation was badly split – soldiers against 'shirkers', peasants against workers, and interventionists against 'defeatists' (as socialists, Catholics and the Giolitti majority in parliament were labelled). The war had also produced other potentially destabilising developments: a more industrialised northern economy, mounting peasant demands for land and growing criticism of the liberal political system. Italy may have emerged victorious in 1918 but could it avoid a post-war crisis?

Activity: The impact of the First World War on Italy

Create a chart to show the strengths and weaknesses of Italy in the period 1915–18 using the following headings: Political, Economic, Social, Military. Record the strengths in the top half and the weaknesses in the bottom half of your chart.

Use your notes on this chapter to answer the following exam question:
Did involvement in the First World War have a positive or negative impact on Italy?

Glossary

Industrial mobilisation system

State-led economic planning designed to maximise production for the war effort.

Inflationary price rises

Inflation occurs when the amount of money and credit in an economy increases relative to the supply of goods and services, and this leads to rising prices. Due to inflation, prices quadrupled between 1913 and 1918.

Agricultural co-operatives

A collective agricultural enterprise where the farmers involved pool their resources and share the rewards which come from their work.

Taking it further

Try to find out more about Italy's participation in the First World War. There is a good chapter on the subject in Martin Clark, *Modern Italy: 1871 to the Present* (3rd edition 2008, pages 217–243). Another interesting account can be found in Christopher Duggan, *The Force of Destiny: A History of Italy since 1796* (2007, pages 390–404).

Chapter 5 The post-war crisis

Key questions

- Why did many Italians see their victory as 'mutilated'?
- What were the main economic problems facing Italy after 1918?
- How did changes to the electoral system undermine the post-war Liberal state?

The end of the First World War did not bring peace and stability to Italy. After 1918, successive governments struggled to deal with three fundamental problems which undermined the Liberal state and paved the way for a fascist dictatorship under Benito Mussolini. The first issue was Italy's failure to secure all its territorial demands at the Paris Peace Conference. Disenchantment with the post-war settlement created a mood of national resentment which was directed at the Entente and the Liberal state. The second issue rose from the difficult transition to a peacetime economy and the growth of urban and rural discontent, which also served to discredit the early post-war governments. The final issue was the introduction of universal male suffrage and proportional representation, which created a 'mass democracy' that undermined the political foundations of the Liberal state.

Take note

As you read through this section, make a list of the reasons why many Italians were disappointed with the peace settlement. Was Italy treated badly by the Entente Powers?

Timeline

December 1918	Universal male suffrage introduced in Italy
January 1919	Catholic Popular Party (PPI) founded
June 1919	Francesco Nitti became prime minister; Food riots in northern and central Italy
August 1919	Party list electoral system (and proportional representation) introduced
September 1919	Treaty of Saint Germain signed; D'Annunzio occupied Fiume
October 1919	Socialist Party's annual congress endorsed policy of revolution
November 1919	First general election held under new electoral system; Liberals and their allies lost control of the Chamber
June 1920	Giovanni Giolitti became prime minister
November 1920	Treaty of Rapallo between Italy and Yugoslavia signed
December 1920	Italian government ends occupation of Fiume by force

'Mutilated victory'

The nationalist writer Gabriele D'Annunzio (see page 21) coined the phrase 'mutilated victory' to express the widely held view in Italy that the country had not received its just rewards at the Paris Peace Conference.

The 'mutilated victory'

Italy and the peace settlement

Italy's victory exacted a high price. Some 600,000 men had been killed and almost 1 million seriously wounded. Much now depended on the Italian government securing a favourable peace settlement but Italy's delegates at the 1919 peace conference, Prime Minister Orlando and Foreign Secretary Sidney Sonnino, were in a difficult position. At home, D'Annunzio and other interventionists and nationalists had whipped up public opinion to expect extensive territorial gains, including the Adriatic port of Fiume which had not been mentioned in the 1915 Treaty of London. Orlando warned that

Italian popular feeling was 'very excitable' and that the 'consequences of a disappointment would be very grave'. Britain, France and the USA, however, did not regard Italy as an equal and considered its demands excessive.

In the Entente's view, Italy's modest contribution to the war effort did not merit such generous rewards. Privately, the head of the British Foreign Office dismissed the Italian representatives as 'odious colleagues' who whined and sulked. There were other problems too. Orlando and Sonnino argued that the territorial claims set out in the 1915 Treaty of London (South Tyrol, the Trentino, Istria and parts of Dalmatia) should be honoured. This agreement had remained secret and the signatories had not informed Woodrow Wilson, the US president, about its contents. By the end of the First World War, however, it was widely accepted by the Entente that the peace settlement would be based on **President Wilson's 'Fourteen Points'**.

Three of these points – calling for open diplomacy, Italy's borders to be adjusted along nationalist lines and the peoples of Austria-Hungary to develop autonomy – contradicted the Treaty of London. When the **Treaty of Saint Germain** was eventually signed in September 1919, Italy fared well, receiving the Trentino, South Tyrol (which included 200,000 German-speaking Austrians), Trieste, Istria and Eastern Galicia. The dissolution of the Austro-Hungarian Empire also removed Italy's chief rival in the area. Overseas, Italy extended her Libyan possessions and obtained a small part of Somaliland from Britain.

Italy in 1920

Treaty of Saint Germain (1919)

This treaty was drawn up at the Paris Peace Conference to settle matters between the Entente and Austria. It dismantled the Austro-Hungarian Empire and former imperial territory was given to Italy, Romania and the 'successor states' (Czechoslovakia, Poland and Yugoslavia). Austria became a small independent republic and was barred from forming an economic or political union with Germany. The Entente concluded a separate settlement, the Treaty of Trianon (1920), with Hungary.

What Italy wanted	Promised in the 1915 Treaty of London?	Delivered by the 1919 Treaty of Saint Germain?
South Tyrol	Yes	Yes
Trentino	Yes	Yes
Istria	Yes	Yes
Fiume	No	No
Dalmatia	Yes	No
German colonies	Yes	No

Italy and the 1919 peace settlement

President Wilson's 'Fourteen Points'

Woodrow Wilson was the US President from 1913 to 1921 and, in April 1917, he took the USA into the First World War on the Entente side. In January 1918 he outlined his 'Fourteen Points' for a post-war settlement which advocated, among other things, open diplomacy, freedom of the seas, international free trade, universal disarmament, national self-determination and a 'league of nations' to preserve peace. Wilson's Fourteen Points became the unofficial war aims of the Entente Powers but they were only partially applied at the Paris Peace Conference due to political self-interest and complex ethnic divisions. The US Senate refused to ratify the resulting Treaty of Versailles.

Francesco Nitti

(1868–1953)

A professor of economics and Radical Party member, Nitti served as minister of finance (1917–19) before becoming prime minister (1919–20). Afterwards, he continued to serve in parliament until 1924. Nitti strongly opposed Mussolini and fascism and, from the mid-1920s, he was forced to live in exile in France. He did not return to Italy until after the Second World War, serving as a senator in 1948.

Gabriele D'Annunzio and Italian legionaries occupy Fiume

Yet many Italians, not just nationalists and interventionists, denounced the peace settlement. They claimed that the Entente had undermined Italy's victory for their own selfish or self-righteous motives, and the Italian government had failed to defend the nation's vital interests. Certainly, Britain and France had made greater sacrifices during the war and were not in a giving mood after being compelled to send military reinforcements in 1917 to shore up the Italian front. President Wilson also refused several Italian demands, notably for Fiume and Dalmatia, because they infringed the principle of national self-determination. To make matters worse, Orlando failed to press the Italian case effectively. He was no match for his British and French counterparts, the crafty David Lloyd George and the hard-headed Georges Clemenceau.

The Entente decided that Fiume, with its mixed Italian and Croat population, and the Dalmatian coast, which was ethnically Slav, should go to newly created Yugoslavia. On hearing this news, Orlando broke down and wept. France, in particular, wanted a strong Yugoslavia as part of a chain of new central European states which would prevent Germany expanding eastward in the future. Italy was also denied a share of Turkey and Germany's African colonies. Demobilised soldiers, particularly ex-officers, regarded the peace settlement as scant reward for their efforts. As they saw it, liberal democracy was failing to translate their vision of a dynamic expansionist Italy into reality, and the anti-war Socialist Party was threatening to take control.

The occupation of Fiume

In September 1919, some 2000 soldiers (mostly deserters and mutineers) led by Gabriele D'Annunzio seized Fiume in defiance of the Italian government. This military takeover had been organised by nationalists, senior army officers and sympathetic industrialists. The occupation was achieved without any violence because General Pittaluga, commander of the local Italian troops, refused to stop D'Annunzio's men, and the Italians living in Fiume enthusiastically welcomed their 'liberators'. That so many troops deserted to join this venture, and Pittaluga offered no resistance, clearly revealed how the Italian military felt about Fiume in particular and the 'mutilated victory' in general. D'Annunzio and his self-styled 'legionaries' became national heroes because, with one bold act, they had succeeded where months of official diplomacy had failed. It was clear that the new government of **Francesco Nitti** (which had replaced Orlando's administration in June 1919) lacked the resolve to use the army against D'Annunzio's forces because the occupation was very popular in Italy. In fact, Fiume was held against the wishes of the Italian authorities, the Western allies and Yugoslavia (where the port was located), for over a year. D'Annunzio declared Fiume an independent republic and, as its 'Regent', conducted numerous nationalist ceremonies and rallies. A constitution was introduced, a newspaper was founded and a local militia established. He also hoped to use Fiume as a base from which to launch a march on Rome.

Nitti's successor, Giovanni Giolitti, who became prime minister in June 1920, took a much firmer line. He effectively marginalised D'Annunzio by negotiating the Treaty of Rapallo (November 1920) with Yugoslavia. Under the terms of the treaty, Italy received the whole of Istria and Italian speakers in Dalmatia could choose to become Italian citizens. Fiume was made an independent city under international control. D'Annunzio refused to accept this settlement and rashly declared war on Italy. In December 1920, on Giolitti's orders, an Italian battleship shelled D'Annunzio's palace and troops stormed the port. 52 died in the fighting and, after four days, D'Annunzio and his legionaries surrendered. Keen to avoid damaging publicity, the government never put him on trial for seizing the port.

Fiume proved to be an important episode for several reasons. Most obviously, popular acclaim for the takeover revealed the extent of Italian dissatisfaction with the post-war settlement. Indeed, many Italians regarded Giolitti's successful attempt to end the occupation as an act of national betrayal. The seizure of Fiume also exposed the weakness of the Italian state and revealed that the loyalty of the Italian army could not be taken for granted. It seemed to demonstrate too that direct action could achieve rapid results by circumventing the traditional political methods of negotiation and compromise. Finally, as Fiume's 'Regent', D'Annunzio developed a new style of mass politics which included forcing opponents to drink castor oil, giving the 'Roman salute', chanting slogans and making balcony speeches to enthusiastic crowds below. Mussolini visited Fiume during the occupation and these techniques heavily influenced his approach to fascism.

The post-war economic crisis

The economic aftermath of the First World War

The Liberal state came under further pressure as its economic difficulties mounted in the immediate post-war period. To fund the war effort, the government had borrowed heavily from Britain and the USA. As a result, Italy's national debt rose from 16 billion to 85 billion lire between 1914 and 1919. Since these loans did not fully cover Italy's war expenditure, the government had also printed more money which, in turn, created soaring inflation. By 1920, the lira was worth just 25% of its 1914 value and, between 1915 and 1921, the cost of living quadrupled. Inflation eroded middle-class savings, landowners' rents, state pensions, and real wages for state employees and factory workers. Large industrial companies, such as FIAT and Pirelli, had made enormous profits due to wartime government contracts but, after 1918, demand for their products fell significantly as the authorities imposed spending cuts. With orders drying up, industrial share prices halved and in 1921 two major munitions companies, Ansaldo and Ilva, collapsed.

A militant workforce

After 1918, industrialists also had to contend with a more militant workforce. Once wartime factory discipline was eased, workers protested in increasing numbers against falling living standards, long hours and the strike ban.

Glossary

Price index

The price index measures price level changes over time. For example, if the food price index rises from 100 to 120 over twelve months then food prices have increased by 20 per cent during the year.

Take note

As you read through this section, identify the main reasons for the growth of militancy in urban and rural areas. How effectively did the government respond to popular discontent?

Price index	
1913	100
1918	413
1920	591

Lira to the £	
Mar 1919	30
Dec 1920	100

Key economic factors

Catholic trade unions

These were non-socialist trade unions organised by the Catholic-controlled *Confederazione Italiana del Lavoro* (Italian Confederation of Labour) or CIL.

Staple

Basic dietary foods essential for well-being.

Sharecropping

A system of agriculture in which a landowner permits a tenant (sharecropper) to cultivate land in return for a share of the crop produced on it.

Take note

As you read through this section, identify the problems that the new 'mass democracy' caused the Liberal state and the ways in which the Socialist and Popular Parties destabilised the political system.

In 1914, a total of 170,000 workers had participated in 781 strikes. Five years later, 1.5 million were involved in 1860 stoppages and in 1920 there were nearly 2 million strikers. Manual workers also flocked to the socialist trade unions, boosting their membership from 250,000 to 2 million between 1918 and 1920. A further 1.2 million employees, mainly engaged in textile production and agriculture, belonged to **Catholic trade unions**. Returning soldiers, who possessed only small discharge payments, were angry about their poor job prospects in the post-war economic downturn. By late 1919, unemployment had climbed to 2 million and there was severe social unrest. According to Sir George Buchanan, the British ambassador in Rome, the situation had become so volatile, particularly in the north, that some regions were barely under government control.

Middle-class Italians and conservatives, fearful of a socialist revolution, expected the authorities to deal harshly with the workers, but the government, in their view, failed to respond decisively. Often the official reaction was to pacify strikes and riots with compromises and favourable settlements. Nitti's ministry urged industrialists to make concessions to their employees, and also established food committees to control supplies and prices after riots broke out in northern and central Italy in June 1919 over the soaring price of **staple** items. Italian shopkeepers bitterly resented this intervention because it halved the price of many of the basic foods they sold. In the short-term, these government attempts to 'buy off' popular discontent were successful but they left the middle classes deeply alienated.

Discontent in the countryside

Simmering economic and social tension was also evident in the rural areas, not least because demobilised soldiers returned to their villages demanding 'land to the peasants'. Many of them bought land from intimidated or financially strapped landowners. Others took over uncultivated areas by force, particularly in Latium (around Rome) and the south. Overall, between 1911 and 1921, the number of peasant owners doubled to around 3.5 million. Land purchases and occupations took place in northern and central Italy too. Peasant **sharecroppers** in Tuscany and Umbria, for instance, clamoured for full ownership, the right to retain more of the produce and greater influence over land use. Moreover, a socialist trade union strike campaign on behalf of agricultural labourers in Emilia (who were hired on a casual basis by tenant farmers in the region) pressed for better wages, jobs for members only and a guarantee of winter work. In the left-wing strongholds of Ferrara and Bologna, the socialist unions' labour exchanges controlled agricultural jobs and wages and prohibited the hiring of non-union workers.

Faced with these challenges, the larger landowners and tenant farmers felt beleaguered. Government measures merely strengthened their resentment. Official decrees passed in 1919 and 1920 recognised peasant occupations of uncultivated land and endorsed union labour exchanges. The latter were given state subsidies as well. Many landowners concluded that the government was actively encouraging revolution in the countryside.

Growing political instability

Italy becomes a mass democracy

Italy's unstable political system was the other factor fuelling the post-war crisis. The First World War had split the traditional ruling elite into hostile factions. Interventionists opposed neutralists and Giolitti's supporters vied with Salandra's followers. Divisions also existed within the ranks of the so-called '**democratic interventionists**', whose aims had been thwarted at the 1919 peace conference. In addition, the Liberal state made changes to the electoral system that were to have far-reaching political consequences.

- In December 1918, Orlando introduced universal male suffrage for all Italians (irrespective of age) who had served at the front and every other man over the age of 21. This measure, designed to reward the troops, created an Italian electorate of 11 million.

- Then, eight months later, the Nitti government opted for **proportional representation** by bringing in the **party list system**. Under these new arrangements, Italy was divided into 54 enormous constituencies and would elect 508 deputies.

The advent of mass democracy and the shift to proportional representation undermined the importance of the traditional link between liberal politicians and the local elites who kept them in power. The future belonged to parties with the resources and machinery to organise mass voter support at elections. At the time, however, few shared the shrewd assessment of Giovanni Amendola, a journalist and liberal politician, that 'the list system means the abdication of the Liberal Party'.

The impact of the Socialist and Catholic Parties

The radicalisation and growth of the Socialist Party (PSI) compounded the regime's political problems. Inspired by the Bolshevik Party's seizure of power in Russia in 1917, the PSI executive adopted a policy of revolution in December 1918. This decision was endorsed by the party's annual congress in October the following year. Furthermore, the PSI joined the **Comintern** and sent high-level representatives to the Soviet Union. Now committed to a socialist republic and the dictatorship of the proletariat – or manual labourers – the Socialist Party organised numerous strikes, protests and demonstrations in Italy. It attracted huge support too, with membership increasing from 50,000 to 200,000 between 1914 and 1919.

In reality, however, much of the PSI's radicalism was for show. The party had no clear strategy for carrying out a socialist revolution and focused instead on preparing for the November 1919 general election. Nevertheless, the Socialist Party's radical image and its encouragement of workers' protests destabilised the political system in two important ways.

Glossary

Democratic interventionists

The collective name given to a moderate pro-war faction that included republicans, radicals and reformist socialists. They hoped that victory in the war would lead to social progress and a more democratic political system in Italy. They called for a peace settlement firmly based on President Wilson's Fourteen Points but were discredited when this failed to materialise.

Proportional representation (PR)

An electoral system in which the percentage of the seats held by a political party in the Chamber closely matches the percentage of the popular vote it received.

Party list system

Under this PR system, voters choose parties not candidates. Parliamentary seats are awarded in proportion to the votes received.

Comintern

The Communist International or Third International, a Moscow-based organisation set up by Lenin in 1919. It aimed to co-ordinate and control the activities of national communist parties and spread communist revolution throughout the world.

Glossary

Non-confessional

This meant that the PPI's programme did not include policies on Church–state relations and did not call for religious laws.

1919 election
508 Deputies

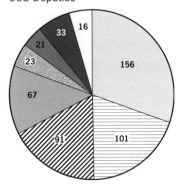

1921 election
522 Deputies

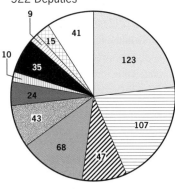

▨ PSI
▤ PPI
▨ Giolittians
▨ Radicals
▨ Right Liberals
▨ Reformist Socialists
▨ Nationalists
■ Fascists
▨ Slavs/Germans
▨ PCI (Communists)
■ War Veterans
☐ Others

For one thing, it meant that the PSI could not be drawn into coalition governments with 'bourgeois' parties. Secondly, it meant that the Italian middle classes, fearful of an imminent left-wing uprising, became increasingly disenchanted with the liberal state's apparent failure to crush socialist subversion.

The creation of a mass Catholic party pledged to 'combat capitalistic liberalism' placed extra pressure on Italy's political system. In 1918, Pope Benedict XV granted Catholics permission to participate in national elections and, in January 1919, the Catholic Popular Party (PPI) was founded under the leadership of Luigi Sturzo. Backed chiefly by peasant owners and tenants in the northern half of the country, the PPI endorsed (and often organised) their land and rent campaigns. Moreover, although the PPI was officially '**non-confessional**' and did not seek to represent the Church's interests, most of its supporters were practising Catholics who rejected the secular Liberal state and the landlords. Consequently, the emergence of the PPI in the immediate post-war period made it harder for liberal politicians to win over and retain Catholic opinion at the very time when such support was needed to ensure that the political system continued to function. In fact, no government during this period was able to secure the long-term allegiance of the PPI.

The end of the Liberal state

When the first elections under the new rules were held in **November 1919**, the results demonstrated that the Liberal state had effectively collapsed. The PSI and the PPI, the two organised mass parties, obtained 156 and 101 seats respectively. Between them, they accounted for over half the vote, with the Socialists taking 32.4% and the Popular Party 20.5%. The liberals (and their allies) won 220 seats but lost control of parliament. Elections in 1921 produced a similar result. From this point on, liberal governments required either Socialist or Catholic support in order to survive. Stable coalition ministries proved elusive, however, and between 1919 and 1922, Italy had four different **prime ministers**.

In short, the post-war Italian democratic system contributed significantly to political instability because it undermined the customary practice of *trasformismo* and led to the emergence of mass parties which were either unwilling or unable to form lasting coalition governments.

Three key factors made parliamentary politics unstable in the immediate post-war years.

● First, the liberals were unable to form a majority administration on their own. In clinging to the pre-war methods of *trasformismo*, they failed to act as a unified party and come to terms with the new mass democracy.

● Second, the PSI, now formally advocating socialist revolution and the destruction of the bourgeois parliamentary system, refused to co-operate with non-socialist parties and would not serve in a coalition government. This strategy was designed to subvert liberal democracy.

Finally, for the system to function without the Socialists, the liberals and the PPI had to work together. Unfortunately, there was little common ground on many issues. Anti-clerical liberals refused to make concessions over Catholic schools, female suffrage and agrarian reform as the price for ongoing PPI support in parliament. These liberal–Catholic conflicts led to protracted government crises which eroded public confidence in the parliamentary system.

Conclusion: A system in crisis?

By 1920–21 Liberal Italy was a state in crisis. For many Italians, it had failed to obtain the kind of territorial rewards due to a victorious nation after the First World War. Indeed, D'Annunzio's daring occupation of Fiume seemed to underline the government's weakness in pressing its case for greater concessions. The transition to peacetime conditions had also created serious economic difficulties and sharpened social divisions which undermined the liberal system. In particular, growing working-class militancy during these years led 'respectable' Italians to fear an immediate socialist revolution. At the same time, changes to the electoral system, and the emergence of the PSI and the PPI, made it virtually impossible to form stable coalition ministries. Fascism proved to be the one political force capable of exploiting these circumstances, first to build up a support base and then to acquire power.

Activity: What was wrong with post-war Italy?

Divide into five groups. Each group should choose one of the following topics:
- the 'mutilated victory'
- Fiume
- economic developments during and after the First World War (to 1920–21)
- the 1919 election
- the rise of worker militancy in the immediate post-war period.

Each group should research its topic using this chapter (and other resources) and then present its findings to the rest of the class. The presentation should cover the following:

(a) a brief description of the event or development

(b) how it weakened the Liberal state

(c) how it could be seen as the most important factor undermining post-war Italy.

Alternatively, imagine you are one of the following living in Italy between 1918 and 1920:
- one of D'Annunzio's followers at Fiume
- an industrial worker
- a middle-class Italian
- a peasant.

Write a short letter (no more than one side of A4 paper) to a friend or relative explaining how you feel about the state of post-war Italy.

Prime minister	Period in office
Francesco Nitti	June 1919–June 1920
Giovanni Giolitti	June 1920–June 1921
Ivanoe Bonomi	June 1921–February 1922
Luigi Facta	February 1922–October 1922

Italian prime ministers, 1919–22

Taking it further

Try to find out more about the post-war crisis in Italy. An excellent account can be found in John Hite and Chris Hinton, *Fascist Italy* (1998), pages 26–35. This commentary is well illustrated, clearly set out and asks some interesting questions about the period. Another good survey is available in Alexander De Grand, *Italian Fascism: Its Origins and Development* (1982), pages 22–29.

Chapter 6 **The rise of Italian fascism: 1919–22**

Key questions
- What did Italian fascism stand for?
- How did the fascist movement operate before achieving power?
- What was Mussolini's role in the rise of Italian fascism?
- Who supported the fascist movement and why?

Between 1919 and 1922, growing disillusionment with the Liberal state and fear of a Socialist takeover transformed Italian fascism from a tiny fringe organisation into an influential mass movement. During this period, Benito Mussolini, the fascist leader, pursued a dual policy to secure power. A key aspect of this strategy was a campaign of fascist violence and intimidation against the Socialists and Communists. Such action was designed to highlight the supposed left-wing threat, expose the Liberal state's lack of authority, persuade Italians that only the fascists could maintain order and coerce the political establishment into making concessions. At the same time, Mussolini also attempted to keep the conventional route to power open. He posed as a responsible leader and assured prominent liberal politicians that the fascist movement would act constitutionally and respect the parliamentary system. This twin-track approach culminated in the 'March on Rome' of October 1922, which brought Mussolini to power.

Take note

As you read through this section, make a list of the key features of Italian fascism in 1919. Why did Mussolini move to the right after the 1919 general election?

Timeline

March 1919	*Fasci di Combattimento* founded
November 1919	Italian fascist movement failed to win a single parliamentary seat at the general election
July 1920	Fascist violence in Trieste
September 1920	Worker occupation of factories
November 1920	Socialists performed well in regional elections
January 1921	Italian Communist Party (PCI) formed
May 1921	Italian fascist movement joined Giolitti's 'National Block' for the general election
August 1921	Benito Mussolini signed the 'Pact of Pacification' with the parliamentary PSI and the General Confederation of Labour
November 1921	National Fascist Party (PNF) founded; Mussolini abandoned the 'Pact of Pacification'
July 1922	24-hour general strike called by socialist trade unions, republicans and radicals
October 1922	Fascist 'March on Rome' planned and carried out; Mussolini became prime minister

Founding the fascist movement

The origins and characteristics of fascism

The term 'fascism' originated in Italy and derived from the word *fasces*, a bundle of sticks that symbolised imperial authority and unity during the Roman Empire. Fascist movements emerged in Europe after 1918 as a response to a number of factors: first, the failure of post-war parliamentary regimes to solve serious social and economic problems; second, the communist seizure of power in Russia in 1917; and, third, the collapse of the great European empires at the end of the First World War.

Unlike Marxism, fascism never developed into a coherent political philosophy. Nevertheless, although they exhibited different features, the various fascist movements which appeared in Italy, Germany and elsewhere did share a number of common characteristics:

- extreme nationalism
- hostility towards communism and socialism
- commitment to one-party rule
- rejection of parliamentary democracy
- belief in a powerful leader or dictator
- desire to control all aspects of life within a totalitarian state.

The *Fasci di Combattimento* (1919)

By February 1919, around 20 ex-servicemen's leagues had been established in places such as Milan, Venice, Naples, Florence and Ferrara. In March 1919, at Benito Mussolini's urging, their representatives, and other pro-war figures, gathered in Milan to launch a new movement, the *Fasci di Combattimento* or 'Combat Group'.

Between 100 and 120 representatives attended, including **Arditi**, interventionist syndicalists, futurists and republicans. Little united these groups beyond a common hostility towards the Liberal state and the Socialists' class war propaganda. Mussolini gave a speech attacking the PSI and Russian **Bolshevism**, extolling the nation's victory in the war and calling for an Italian Empire. The *Fasci di Cambattimento* aimed to attract the **'trenchocracy'** by stressing it was an activist movement, not a party. The first group was formed in Milan and, within six months, there were branches in most major Italian cities. In June 1919, the movement published its programme, which had a distinctly republican-syndicalist flavour: abolition of the monarchy, a National Assembly, universal suffrage, proportional representation, an eight-hour working day, workers' representatives in industrial management, confiscation of war profits and Church property, and Italy to take possession of Fiume and Dalmatia.

Glossary

Arditi

First World War Italian elite commando troops whose name meant 'the daring ones'. Formed in the summer of 1917, *Arditi* units were specially trained, undertook high-risk missions and acquired a glamorous military reputation. They were often given the task of penetrating enemy defences before the launch of a general infantry assault. Although the *Arditi* were formally demobilised by 1920, D'Annunzio's followers during the occupation of Fiume (1919–20) also adopted the name.

Bolshevism

The Bolsheviks were the revolutionary socialist party who overthrew the Russian government in 1917 and brought about the first successful communist seizure of power.

Trenchocracy

Mussolini argued that the 'trenchocracy' (the servicemen who fought between 1915 and 1918) formed a new class which had been forged by the common experience of war. In his view, only they had the moral right and strength of will to exercise power in post-war Italy.

Fascist squad in 1930

The attack on *Avanti!*

In April 1919, the PSI held a large demonstration in Milan which led to clashes with some 200–300 *Fasci di Cambattimento* members, who then destroyed the offices of *Avanti!* Four people died (including three Socialists) and 39 were wounded. Mussolini played no part in this act of aggression but he later praised the fascists for the attack and accepted 'all moral responsibility' for their conduct. The government did not prosecute any of the fascists involved in the assault. Mussolini concluded that the authorities were prepared to condone anti-socialist violence because they feared left-wing revolution.

The November 1919 election

Neither the *Fasci*'s programme nor its early use of force translated into votes, however. At the November 1919 general election, fascist candidates failed to win a single parliamentary seat. Collectively, the 17 fascist candidates (including Mussolini) in Milan obtained only 4657 of the 270,000 votes cast there, less than 2% of the total. Once the results were known, Mussolini's socialist opponents staged a mock funeral to 'bury' their former colleague and *Avanti!* gloated over his 'political corpse'. After this electoral setback, national membership of the *Fasci* fell to about 4000. Yet, within 12 months, the government's failure to persuade mainstream Italian society that it could neutralise the perceived socialist threat had transformed the fascists' political fortunes.

Mussolini responded to the election result by moving cautiously to the Right. At the second Fascist National Congress in May 1920, he announced that the movement opposed the 'anti-Italian' PSI but not the proletariat (working class), endorsed employer–worker collaboration and called for better relations with the Vatican. The new fascist programme also abandoned earlier pledges to abolish the Senate and confiscate 'excessive' war profits.

Take note

As you read through this section, identify the main reasons for the growth of *squadrismo* and list the reasons why Mussolini became the leader of the fascist movement.

The Liberal state and the rise of fascism 1920–21

The occupation of the factories, September 1920

Widely discredited because of the Fiume episode, Nitti eventually resigned in June 1920. His successor, Giolitti, formed another unstable coalition government but the real problems lay outside parliament. In September 1920, a wage dispute in the engineering industry quickly escalated into a mass 'factory occupation' in the northern cities involving some 400,000 workers. Mussolini carefully kept his options open, welcoming the workers' attempt to secure better economic conditions but also warning against any 'Bolshevik' assault on power.

Angry industrialists pressed the authorities to discipline the workers. Giolitti, however, refused to use force, fearing this would lead to widespread violence and bloodshed. In his view, the occupation would soon collapse on its own. Employers were further incensed when the prime minister urged them to grant concessions (wage rises and worker participation in factory management). In addition, after it emerged that some occupied factories were making weapons, many conservative Italians were convinced that left-wing revolution was imminent. In the event, the occupation petered out within a month, but employers and conservatives never forgave Giolitti for not taking direct action. Furthermore, regional elections in November 1920, which left the socialists in control of 26 of Italy's 69 provinces, raised fears that the left would now increase local taxes for non-manual workers. Small traders also resented the growth of socialist-backed co-operative shops.

Growing rural discontent

Agrarian strikes and land occupations left landowners and rural employers bitterly disillusioned with the government too. By April 1920, about 27,000 hectares of farmland had been seized – mainly by socialist peasant leagues – and handed over to workers' co-operatives. In Catholic areas, PPI unions did much the same thing. The authorities did not intervene, partly because peasant war veterans were legally entitled to uncultivated agricultural land. Up to one-third of hay, grain and grape output in 1920 was lost due to rural strikes and arson attacks. Socialist trade unions began to monopolise agricultural jobs in Emilia, the Po Valley, Umbria and Tuscany. Many unions were also demanding better wages and greater job security for farm labourers. The estates of anti-union landowners were often targeted and their farm managers assaulted. When the November 1920 local elections produced socialist victories in Emilia-Romagna and Tuscany, and a strong PPI performance in Venetia, Lombardy and Piedmont, tensions in rural Italy came to a head.

Squadrismo: The impact of fascist political violence

Organised squads – or *squadristi* – transformed the *Fasci* into a large-scale movement. Towards the end of 1920, the rural Right in northern and central Italy began to fight back against the socialists and the PPI. It was this reaction that gave the *squadristi* and fascism mass support. Feeling abandoned by the government, landowners and middle-class conservatives turned to local fascist groups to avert social revolution. These fascist squads were modelled on military units and each one was led by a **ras**, usually a former officer. At the start, the squads contained mostly ex-army officers and middle-class students but they quickly attracted new recruits. Hostile to left-wing demands for improved wages and land nationalisation, small farmers, farm managers and sharecroppers joined in large numbers. Mussolini declared that the **Blackshirts** had 'launched a guerrilla war' against the socialists.

Over the next few months, fascist squads launched a wave of violent raids across Emilia-Romagna and Tuscany. Funded by landowners and supplied by the military, armed *squadristi* attacked socialists and trade unionists.

Squadrismo

The system of organised fascist gangs or 'squads' that used violence against their political opponents in order to achieve their aims. Fascist squad activity began in Trieste in early 1920 to help the authorities 'Italianise' the area and 'deal' with local Slavs and left-wingers. Equipped by the army and secretly funded by industrialists, these fascist gangs controlled the streets of Trieste and other towns in Venezia Giulia within a few months.

Glossary

Ras

The name given to a squad leader. It was originally the title given to tribal chiefs in Abyssinia.

Blackshirt

Another term for fascist, which referred to the movement's black uniform.

Italo Balbo

(1896–1940)

A convinced interventionist, Balbo commanded an Italian army battalion during the First World War. After joining the fascists in February 1921, he became the Ferrara *ras* and ruthlessly destroyed socialist organisations in the area. He was also the main organiser of the March on Rome in 1922. A daring aviator, Balbo served the fascist regime as minister of aviation (1929–33) before becoming governor-general of Libya (1933–40). Balbo's pioneering transatlantic flights to Brazil and the USA between 1930 and 1933 made him extremely popular in Italy, but Mussolini sent him to Libya to remove him from the limelight. In the late 1930s Balbo criticised Mussolini's anti-Semitic measures and opposed closer relations with Nazi Germany. He was accidentally shot down and killed by Italian anti-aircraft gunners when fighting in North Africa in 1940.

Their victims were often forced to drink castor oil. Local labour movement headquarters were wrecked and socialist and PPI councils were driven from office. The squads also acted as rural strike-breakers. Furthermore, fascists persuaded landowners to make leases or small plots available to peasants and some agricultural workers joined *Fasci*-run syndicates and co-operatives. In the first five months of 1921, fascist–socialist clashes left 207 people dead and 819 injured. By the spring of that year, the Left had been crushed in Emilia-Romagna and Tuscany and these regions became squad strongholds. Having assumed control of Ferrara in a few weeks, **Italo Balbo** – the local *ras* – was able to organise a mass rally of 20,000 fascists when Mussolini made a speech there in April 1921.

Damaging internal divisions compounded the socialists' problems. In January 1921, the revolutionary wing of the PSI, led by prominent left-wingers such as Palmiro Togliatti and Antonio Gramsci, broke away to form the Italian Communist Party (PCI). The radical socialists took this action because the PSI party executive refused to carry out Comintern instructions to abandon elections and concentrate on revolution. Nine months later, the PSI eventually complied with the Comintern's directives and expelled a number of moderate socialists. Those who were forced out then formed the Socialist Unity Party (PSU). There were now four **left-wing parties** in Italian politics.

Left wing parties in 1921

Italian Socialist Party (PSI) Founded in 1892, the PSI was Italy's major socialist party and between October 1919 and January 1921 its membership increased from 71,000 to 220,000. However, the party was soon weakened by internal divisions.

Italian Reformist Socialist Party (PSRI) Formed in 1912 by leading reformists after they were expelled from the PSI, the PSRI remained a minor party.

Italian Communist Party (PCI) In the early 1920s, the PCI was too small to pose a real threat to conservative and propertied interests in Italy (it obtained just 15 seats in the 1921 election) but the very existence of a revolutionary Marxist party was a propaganda gift for the fascists. In the 1924 election, the PCI secured just over 268,000 votes (up one-third on 1921) and 19 seats.

Socialist Unity Party (PSU) Established in 1921 by former PSI reformists who had been expelled for favouring the parliamentary rather than the revolutionary route to socialism. Mussolini made two unsuccessful attempts (in 1922 and 1924) to bring the PSU into his government.

Mussolini's response to *squadrismo*

Mussolini realised that *squadrismo's* rapid rise in central Italy represented a golden opportunity. The fascist squads had emerged largely as a spontaneous response to local conditions under the leadership of local *ras*, such as Italo Balbo (Ferrara), **Roberto Farinacci** (Cremona) and **Dino Grandi** (Bologna), who jealously guarded their independence. For this reason, Mussolini had no real control over the squads. Indeed, many *ras* regarded him as self-serving and untrustworthy.

Mussolini, however, was determined to head this burgeoning movement: *squadrismo* damaged his opponents, diverted attention from Fiume and could enhance his political standing. Consequently, he became the squads' self-appointed national spokesman. He promoted their cause in his newspaper, *The Italian People,* and went on speaking tours to boost squad morale. He also provided new *ras* with funds and pro-fascist military contacts. Without his overall leadership, Mussolini argued, the various regional fascist movements would lack coherence and quarrel amongst themselves. For their part, the *ras* could see some advantages in Mussolini assuming this 'national' role. He was a skilled orator and journalist, with a newspaper at his disposal. He was well connected too. They also concluded that the Milan-based Mussolini could not challenge them in their local strongholds.

Fascism: the parliamentary path to power

Squadrismo turned the *Fasci di Combattimerto* into a mass movement but it was the Giolitti–Mussolini pact which opened up the corridors of power to the fascists. Secret discussions between the two men began in the autumn of 1920. Giolitti calculated that, by bringing the *Fasci* into his coalition, he would neutralise the potential fascist threat, gain an anti-socialist ally and further isolate D'Annunzio. His strategy was to 'tame' fascism by absorbing it into his coalition and to use the movement to weaken his political opponents. He dismissed the fascists as 'fireworks' who would 'make a great deal of noise but only leave smoke behind'. It was to be a costly misjudgment. For Mussolini, collaboration with Giolitti offered an anti-Left alliance and the prospect of fascist deputies in parliament. These negotiations culminated in a formal agreement to stand together as a 'National Block' in the May 1921 general election.

In the run-up to the election, Giolitti's official directives to punish all acts of violence were widely ignored. Many within the police, the judiciary, the military and the provincial middle class were pro-fascist. Prefects were also often sympathetic and even those who were not frequently concluded that official intervention would only intensify the violence. Under these circumstances, attacks and disturbances escalated. Between early April and mid-May, 105 people were killed and 431 injured. In late April, Mussolini vainly attempted to rein in the Blackshirts by warning them that 'if fascism loses its "sense of limit" it will lose its victory'.

At the election, the National Block obtained 275 seats overall, which enabled Giolitti to remain prime minister. The *Fasci di Cambattimenti* fielded 75 candidates and 35 of these, including Mussolini, were elected. The 1921 result was a significant setback for the prime minister because almost half of the deputies returned – 123 Socialists, 15 Communists and 107 PPI – were anti-Giolitti. Immediately after the election, Mussolini withdrew the fascists from the National Block. The pact had served its purpose in giving him a parliamentary seat, greater authority and a respectable image. Giolitti managed to form a coalition administration without the fascist deputies but resigned in June 1921 when the PPI refused to support the government.

Biography

Roberto Farinacci

(1892–1945)

PNF general secretary in 1925–26, Farinacci was disliked by most of the other senior fascists, including Mussolini. Restored to power in 1935, he emerged as the leader of the anti-Semitic and pro-German faction of the PNF. He was shot by Italian partisans (anti-fascist resistance fighters) in 1945.

Dino Grandi

(1895–1988)

A rival for the fascist leadership in 1921, Grandi was appointed foreign minister in 1929. He subsequently served as Italian ambassador in London and minister of justice. He opposed Italy's entry into the Second World War and was a key participant in the revolt against the *Duce* in 1943.

Take note

As you read through this section, identify the reasons why Mussolini and Giolitti were prepared to negotiate with each other. Who got the most out of the National Block agreement? What problems were caused by the Pact of Pacification for Mussolini and the fascist movement?

Biography

Ivanoe Bonomi

(1873–1951)

One of the founders of the moderate Reformist Socialist Party in 1912, after he was dismissed from the Socialist Party, Bonomi supported Italy's entry into the First World War. He held several ministerial positions before serving as prime minister from July 1921 to February 1922. An anti-fascist, Bonomi was also prime minister in 1944–45 after the liberation of Rome.

Once elected, Mussolini rarely attended the Chamber and the fascist deputies consciously flouted its 'gentlemanly' traditions. They occupied seats on the extreme Right and forcibly ejected a Communist MP for his alleged 'desertion' during the First World War. In June 1921, Mussolini delivered his first speech in the Chamber. His address condemned socialism and democracy but also attempted to build bridges with the Vatican by acknowledging that 'the Latin and imperial tradition of Rome is today represented by Catholicism'. Mussolini's subsequent public statements endorsed Church schools and attacked **freemasonry** and divorce. He knew that the fascists could not exercise power if they faced widespread Catholic opposition.

The Pact of Pacification

The new prime minister, **Ivanoe Bonomi**, sponsored peace talks between the rival political groups in order to end the violence. Mussolini participated because he felt that the squads' 'physical force' tactics were becoming counterproductive. In August 1921 Mussolini, the parliamentary PSI and the socialist trade union the General Confederation of Labour signed the Pact of Pacification, but neither the PPI nor the PCI endorsed the agreement. The pact put Mussolini and the *ras* on a collision course.

Mussolini maintained that this initiative had averted a grave crisis and warned that 'If fascism does not follow me, no-one can force me to follow fascism'. His position was clear: the movement could not make progress without a credible national leader. The provincial fascist leaders, however, rejected the pact. Farinacci resigned from the fascist central committee, rather than compromise with 'Bolsheviks'. Grandi, Balbo and other *ras* feared the agreement would destroy their local power bases by ending *squadrismo* and undermine the fascist syndicates. Landowners argued that the pact would revive rural socialism just as the harvest period approached. In July 1921, a meeting of 400 Tuscan *Fasci* in Florence voted against the agreement. A month later, 600 *Fasci* gathered at Bologna and decided to offer D'Annunzio the leadership.

Faced with such opposition, Mussolini resigned from the fascist executive in August, but two things worked in his favour. First, the executive supported both the pact and his leadership. Second, D'Annunzio declined the leadership on the grounds that fascism had become too reactionary. Nevertheless, the *ras* remained defiant and, in September, Balbo and Grandi organised a 'march on Ravenna' by 3000 fascists. Furthermore, violence continued in rural areas, mainly instigated by PCI members and the *squadristi*. The Pact of Pacification had failed, but Mussolini managed to hang on as leader of the fascist movement.

The end of the pact and the formation of the National Fascist Party

To preserve his leadership and the unity of the movement, Mussolini now reversed his position. He blamed the Left and the government for the ongoing violence and praised *squadrismo*.

Mussolini struck a deal with Grandi and Balbo too. Under its terms, he agreed to renounce the Pact of Pacification on condition that the movement became a party. He calculated that a party structure, with its formal hierarchy, discipline and regulations, would give him more control over provincial fascism. At the third Fascist National Congress in November 1921, Mussolini's carefully staged public reconciliation with Grandi defused the issue of the pact and reaffirmed his leadership. The Congress approved the move to a party footing and the *Fasci di Combattimenti* became the National Fascist Party (PNF). Crucially, the PNF's 'New Programme' – which was adopted at the same gathering – placed the *squadristi* under the command of the party leadership not the provincial leaders.

Month	No. *Fasci*	Total members
March	371	80,476
June	1192	204,506
September	1268	213,621
December	1333	218,453

The growth of the fascist movement in 1921

1919	1921
2% of the vote	7% of the vote
No MPs	35 MPs

Fascist performance in elections

The Congress marked an important triumph for the PNF leader because, as the historian Richard Bosworth notes, 'in most senses Mussolini had won a final victory over the *ras*.'

A week later, Mussolini formally withdrew the PNF from the pact. Bonomi reacted by issuing directives to disband all armed organisations, including the squads. Mussolini, though, had already given an order which turned all PNF members into *squadristi* on the assumption that the government would not dare suppress *squadrismo* if it meant, in effect, banning the PNF. As Mussolini suspected, Bonomi was afraid to act. By December, the PNF had 1333 *Fasci* and over 218,000 members. Small wonder then that Mussolini called 1921 the 'year of fascism'.

The New Programme

The New Programme, which was adopted at the third Fascist National Congress, revealed how far fascist policies had moved to the right since 1919. Its main provisions included:

- an unspecified political structure to secure Italy's greatness

- new corporations to encourage national unity and increase production

- the state to preserve political and judicial order

- the Church could 'exercise its spiritual mission'; confiscation of religious property was dropped

- national interests took precedence over individual freedoms

- compulsory military service

- progressive not punitive taxation

- privatisation of nationalised firms

- right to own private property guaranteed

- schools to train Italy's future governing elite and soldiers

- Italy to become 'the upholder of Latin civilisation in the Mediterranean'.

Take note

As you read this section, identify the main urban and rural supporters of fascism and explain their motives for backing the fascists.

This programme had a wide appeal but clearly implied that the state could, and would, override individual rights. Moreover, nothing was said about the defence of democratic government and basic freedoms.

The social composition of the Fascist Party in 1921

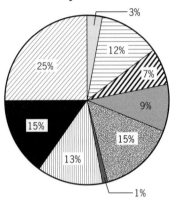

Industrialists
Landowners
Professionals
Tradesmen and artisans
Public and private employees
Teachers
Students
Workers
Agricultural workers

Based on a questionnaire sent out by the PNF in November 1921, which was answered by half the party membership

Who supported the fascist movement?

The early *Fasci* movement that emerged in 1919, with its revolutionary and republican image, was regarded as a 'left-wing' organisation but was unable to compete with the PSI. It attracted, at best, only a few thousand members. These so-called 'fascists of the first hour', typically syndicalists, ex-officers and students, wanted to play an active role in re-establishing Italy as a great power. As fascism moved to the right in 1920–21, many original members departed because they were unhappy with the movement's growing links with conservative interests. Nevertheless, this political shift mobilised important social groups and turned Mussolini's organisation into a mass movement. The major sources of fascist support are identified below. In reality, this more broadly based fascism was a series of local movements which responded to different regional conditions but also shared a common political outlook – patriotism, anti-socialism and recognising the need for strong leadership.

From 1920, small farmers in parts of Romagna, Lombardy and Venetia joined the fascists in large numbers. Having secured, or hoping to acquire, landholdings, the rural **petty bourgeoisie** saw the advance of socialism as a direct threat to their way of life. In response, they turned to fascism for protection. Many small farmers and peasants particularly loathed the trade union-run socialist labour leagues which rigidly controlled agricultural employment. They joined the fascist squads in the belief that, once the labour leagues had been destroyed, jobs, leases and smallholdings would be more widely available. The ***agrari*** reacted against the activities of the labour leagues, the election of left-wing councils and the impact of the government's agricultural policies by backing the fascists too. They funded the fascist squads' campaign of violence against socialist and PPI influence in the countryside in order to defend their own economic and political interests.

Another important source of fascist support from 1920 was the urban petty bourgeoisie, a class which included shopkeepers, artisans, small business owners and merchants, teachers and junior civil servants. Much of the lower-middle class blamed the Liberal state for the damaging impact of inflation, poor post-war job prospects and the failure to stem the growth of socialism. Many ex-servicemen from the petty bourgeoisie also felt the government had not recognised their contribution to Italy's victory in the First World War. Consequently, the fascists, as a nationalist movement opposed to left-wing revolution and the Liberal state, recruited large numbers from the disaffected lower-middle class. Fascism also received support and financial contributions from industrialists who feared the rise of left-wing militancy in the factories and criticised liberal governments for failing to take a hard line against the workers.

Glossary

Petty bourgeoisie

A term often used to describe the lower-middle class.

Agrari

Larger landowners.

Students and youths flocked to the movement and many of them joined the squads. By 1921, about 13% of the country's students belonged to the PNF. For these young Italians, fascism contrasted sharply with the dull routine of their daily lives by offering colour, action and excitement. They also joined to register their resentment of 'unpatriotic' workers and to protest against the difficulty of finding employment after the war.

The fascists attracted working-class support as well. Some Italian workers were attracted by the more radical parts of the fascist programme such as an eight-hour day, employee representatives in management, land for the peasants and fair wages and prices. Others opted for fascism because they detested socialist intimidation of non-unionised labour. Moreover, once the fascists had taken control of areas previously dominated by socialist and PPI unions, many working-class Italians made the pragmatic decision to join the fascist syndicates to ensure they could get a job.

The March on Rome, October 1922

The fascist challenge to the Liberal state

In early 1922, Balbo and General Gandolfo reorganised the squads into a national militia-style force. At the same time, the fascist syndicates were grouped together in a National Confederation of Syndical Corporations. Led by **Edmondo Rossoni**, the National Confederation claimed almost 500,000 members by mid-1922. Publicly, Mussolini endorsed the National Confederation but in private he was concerned about the syndicates, since they were often run by the local *ras* and might discourage funding from sympathetic industrialists.

The Bonomi government collapsed in February 1922 and **Luigi Facta**, an unimpressive liberal compromise candidate, became prime minister. His appointment merely underlined the fact that the parliamentary regime could neither deliver stable government nor impose law and order. The fascists quickly tested the new government by forcibly ejecting the local authorities at Fiume. When Facta took no action, the PNF carried out similar illegal squad 'expeditions' across northern and central Italy during the spring and summer of 1922. They starkly revealed just how little real authority the Liberal state possessed.

- Between May and September, the PNF assumed control of the Po delta by driving out elected socialist councils in the region.

- In June 1922, a fascist occupation of Bologna forced the government to remove the prefect – the local state official – from the city.

Mussolini provided finances and favourable press coverage for these fascist takeovers. By the autumn, the PNF ran much of the upper half of Italy, dominating local government, levying unofficial taxes and controlling the job market through its syndicates.

Take note

As you read through this section, list the weaknesses of the Liberal state in 1922, identify the reasons for the success of Mussolini's dual policy and list the factors that enabled Mussolini to gain office.

Biography

Edmondo Rossoni

(1884–1965)

A former revolutionary syndicalist, Rossoni joined the fascist movement in 1921 and became a member of the Fascist Grand Council. From 1935 to 1939 he served the regime as minister of agriculture and forests.

Luigi Facta

(1861–1930)

Studied law and became a journalist before being elected as a deputy in 1891. A liberal, Facta served in several early twentieth-century coalition governments and by 1919 he had been minister of finance three times and minister of justice. He was the last prime minister of Italy before Mussolini came to power. Facta took over in February 1922 because the other liberal leaders, divided by personal rivalries, were unable to form a coalition government.

Mussolini in militia uniform, with imperial trappings, 1923

Left-wing protest played into Mussolini's hands too. On 31 July 1922, a coalition of moderate socialist trade unions, republicans and radicals held a 24-hour general strike to protest against Fascist brutality and apparent government indifference to squad violence. Relatively few workers participated and fascist-led volunteers quickly defeated the stoppages that did occur. Mussolini used the strike as an effective propaganda weapon, claiming the PNF had restored order and prevented left-wing revolution. Many conservative Italians agreed. The failed stoppage virtually ended organised left-wing anti-fascist protest. Buoyed by their success, the fascists seized control of the Milan and Genoa councils, and ransacked the Milan offices of *Avanti!*. It was now widely assumed that the PNF would have to be offered a role in government.

Mussolini's dual policy

Throughout this period, Mussolini skilfully pursued a dual policy to obtain power which involved playing up the threat of violence and offering assurances to important groups.

The threat of violence

By targeting the socialists and exposing the Liberal state's lack of authority, he hoped to play up the left-wing threat, persuade the middle classes that only the PNF could maintain order, and pressure the political establishment with the prospect of a fascist coup. Such a strategy called for a delicate balancing act. Mussolini knew that direct action by the PNF had to be extensive enough to keep the spectre of 'red revolution' alive and satisfy the squads who wanted a fascist seizure of power. However, he was also well aware that excessive fascist force would alienate potential supporters and might lead to an armed response by the state. His ability to exploit this tactic without splitting his own movement or antagonising conservative Italians was a testimony to his political skill.

Offering assurances: negotiating with liberals

Simultaneously, Mussolini secretly negotiated with key liberal politicians (Orlando, Giolitti, Salandra and Nitti) to assure them the PNF would act constitutionally and accept the parliamentary system. In these discussions, he posed as the responsible leader who could work with the political establishment and discipline the violent party hotheads. This second strand of the policy was designed to allay suspicion, divide political opponents and keep the conventional route to power open. It worked for two reasons. First, the leading liberal politicians seemed more concerned about outmanoeuvring each other than offering a common front against fascism. They were all eager to include the PNF to strengthen their own claims to government. Second, by mid-1922 it was clear that the PNF would have a significant role in the next coalition government. In fact, these meetings were designed to conceal Mussolini's real ambition to become prime minister. They were also motivated by his desire to prevent another Giolitti ministry because Italy's elder statesman might use force against the PNF (as he had against D'Annunzio at Fiume). Mussolini observed tersely: 'If Giolitti returns to power, we're f*****.'

Offering assurances: the army and the king

Mussolini was wary of seizing power by force since this risked conflict with the army. Consequently, he cultivated the support of serving and former officers, and several retired generals advised the PNF. Nevertheless, the vast majority of the senior ranks would not have backed an armed rebellion against the monarch. As commander-in-chief, King Victor Emmanuel III could order the army to suppress the fascists, and, constitutionally, only he could appoint the prime minister. Since the king's attitude was crucial, Mussolini attempted to win him over. In September 1922, he delivered a speech which argued that fascism and the Crown could coexist. Moreover, to increase fascist influence over the king, two royalist sympathisers recruited the Queen Mother to the fascist cause. For good measure, Victor Emmanuel III's cousin, the pro-fascist Duke of Aosta, took up residence near the PNF's headquarters in Perugia. The message was obvious: an alternative ruler was available if the king opposed the fascists.

Planning to take power

On 16 October, Mussolini met PNF militia leaders and other senior Fascists to plan a 'March on Rome'. This decision enabled Mussolini to retain control over the radical fascists and put further pressure on the Italian establishment. Four **quadrumvirs** – Balbo, **Cesare De Vecchi**, **Emilio De Bono** and **Michele Bianchi** – were also appointed to organise and command the march. Discussions about timing were postponed until the PNF congress at Naples, which was scheduled for 24 October. Mussolini knew he had to act quickly because, by Armistice Day (4 November), the capital would be full of parading soldiers loyal to the Crown. At the same time, to keep his options open, Mussolini continued secret negotiations with the liberal factions to form part of a legally constituted government. Once at Naples, the fascist leadership decided to seize the northern and central cities not already under PNF control from midnight on 27 October and then move against Rome the following day.

On that night, PNF squads took over provincial town halls, telephone exchanges, post offices and railway stations whilst 30,000 Blackshirts began assembling at three towns outside Rome in readiness for the march on the capital. During the early hours of 28 October, the Facta government finally acted and persuaded the king to introduce martial law so that the police and the army could counter the Blackshirt threat. The 30,000 lightly armed fascists now faced the prospect of military defeat by the 28,000-strong Rome garrison, which was well trained, better equipped and ably led by General Pugliese. By 9 am that morning, however, Victor Emmanuel III had changed his mind and refused to sign the martial law declaration. His rejection of this unanimous cabinet recommendation breached constitutional convention. It also brought Mussolini and the PNF to power.

Michele Bianchi

(1883–1930)

A journalist and former revolutionary syndicalist leader, Bianchi was a founder member of the fascist movement in 1919. He joined the Fascist Grand Council in 1923 and was appointed minister of public works in 1929. He died from tuberculosis a year later.

Mussolini becomes prime minister

Just why Victor Emmanuel III reversed his decision is not entirely clear but he did not intend to pave the way for a fascist dictatorship. His change of heart was probably due to several factors. Certainly, he resented the incompetence of the parliamentary regime and doubted Facta's ability to handle the crisis. Furthermore, several generals questioned the army's willingness to fire on the fascists because many PNF members were former soldiers and officers. If the king's military orders were disobeyed, he would have to abdicate. Victor Emmanuel III also received inaccurate information, which questioned the army's ability to defend Rome against the assembled Blackshirt forces. Another powerful motive was the monarch's desire to avoid a civil war – particularly with his pro-fascist cousin, the Duke of Aosta, waiting to replace him.

Mussolini surrounded by his government, flanked by Admiral de Revel and Marshall Diaz, having been granted his full powers by the Chamber, November 1922

Denied martial law, the Facta administration resigned. The king then invited Salandra to form a government, but this came to nothing. Without martial law, and unable to secure PNF involvement, Salandra abandoned his attempt to create a coalition government. Mussolini refused to participate because he knew he could become prime minister. In order to thwart his rival Giolitti, Salandra advised Victor Emmanuel to send for the PNF leader, who had returned to Milan. On 29 October the king reluctantly did so and Mussolini made the overnight railway journey to Rome. Waiting for his train at Milan, Mussolini commented 'I want to leave on time. From now on everything must work perfectly'. His remark led to the joke that at least fascism made the trains run on time. On 30 October, Victor Emmanuel appointed the PNF leader prime minister in the usual constitutional manner and accepted his cabinet nominations. Only four of these were fascists.

Within twenty-four hours, the fascist marchers entered the capital – once Pugliese had been ordered to let them through. They then physically attacked political opponents and ran riot in working-class districts. Subsequently, Mussolini's regime recast October 1922 as a heroic myth where, following a bloody civil war, some 300,000 Blackshirts had issued an ultimatum to the king and seized power at the cost of 3000 fascist 'martyrs'. Many fascists at the time genuinely believed they had carried out a revolution, but in truth the 'March on Rome' had been an act of political blackmail which removed the need for a real insurrection.

Conclusion: How did Mussolini come to power?

Mussolini used constitutional and revolutionary methods to become prime minister. Outwardly at least, he achieved office by the traditional route. He was appointed by the king, and his patriotic stance during the First World War and the 'Bolshevik' threat of 1921–22 had garnered support from conservative Italians. Simultaneously, Mussolini also rode the revolutionary wave to power. *The Italian People* gave him a press platform to become the national spokesman for, and the principal political beneficiary of, anti-Versailles opinion and *squadrismo*. In the end, the establishment accepted Mussolini to avoid a damaging domestic conflict. They anticipated that, as prime minister, he would abide by the constitution, curb the radical fascists and provide a temporary solution for Italy's difficulties.

Taking it further

Try to find out more about the rise of Italian fascism between 1919 and 1922. Two contrasting but accessible accounts can be found in Denis Mack Smith, *Mussolini* (1981), pages 35–56 and Nicholas Farrell, *Mussolini: A New Life* (2004), Chapters 7 and 8.

Activity: This house believes…

Historians have disagreed over the extent to which violence and intimidation played a role in Mussolini's appointment as prime minister. Your task is to divide into two teams and formally debate this issue. The first team must propose the motion: 'This house believes that Mussolini became prime minister due to fascist violence and intimidation.' The second team must oppose this motion.

Spend some time preparing for this debate. Use the information in this chapter to find general points and specific examples to support your argument.

Each team should appoint a leader. With the help of the team, the team leader should prepare a five minute speech, outlining the team's argument. An impartial Chair should also be appointed to oversee the debate and award points.

Structure the debate as follows:

1. The two teams should face each other, with the team leaders in central positions.

2. The Chair should introduce the debate and welcome the teams. Invite the team leaders to present their speeches, proposing and opposing the motion.

3. Following the speeches, the floor is opened for contributions (in the form of questions or comments) from the other members of the teams.

4. Points are awarded by the Chair, using the following system:
   - 1 point for each relevant question
   - 2 points for each general statement
   - 5 points for each general statement supported by a specific example.

5. It is the role of the Chair to ensure that politeness is maintained at all times.

6. At the end of the debate, the team with the most points is declared the winner.

Skills Builder 2: **Planning answers to questions on causation and change**

Questions on causation

In the AS examination you may be asked questions on causation – questions about what caused historical events to take place.

Some questions may ask you to explain why something happened. For example:

> (A) Why did support for the Italian fascist movement increase between 1919 and 1922?

Other questions on causation will ask you to assess the importance of one cause of an event in relation to other causes. These often begin with 'How far' or 'To what extent'. Here is an example:

> (B) How far do you agree that the threat of left-wing revolution explains the increasing support for the Italian fascist movement between 1919 and 1922?

Planning your answer

Before you write your essay you need to make a plan. In the exam you will have to do this very quickly! The first thing to do is to identify the key points you will make in your answer. Let's look at some examples.

When planning an answer to Question (A) you need to note down reasons why support for the Italian fascist movement increased. You can do this in the form of a list or a concept map.

When planning an answer to Question (B) you need to think about the importance of each reason. You could:

- write a list of all the reasons then number them in order of importance
- draw a concept map with 'increasing support for the Italian fascist movement' at the centre, and put the most important reasons near the middle and the least important reasons further away.

It is much easier to assess the importance of one factor when you have a list of all the relevant factors in front of you!

The information you require for these answers can be found in Chapters 5 and 6. Go to Chapters 5 and 6 and identify the reasons for growing fascist support.

Linking the causes

Once you have identified the relevant information and organised it, it is important to highlight links between the reasons.

In making your plan, try grouping reasons together which have links. If you have produced a list of reasons, you may want to rearrange the points where you can identify clear links between them. If you have drawn a concept map, you could draw arrows between the linked points.

Writing your answer

For Question (A) above, you could write a paragraph on each cause. Alternatively, you might want to start with what you think is the most important cause and then deal with the other causes.

For Question (B) above, it is essential that you refer to the relative importance of different causes, focusing particularly on the 'threat of left-wing revolution'. Remember to answer the question! You might want to deal with the threat of left-wing revolution first and then assess the importance of other points explaining the increase in support for the Italian fascist movement. Make sure you write a separate paragraph for each reason that you identify.

Questions about change

These questions will require you to explain how far a specified factor changed during a historical period.

Examples of this type of question would be:

> (C) How far did the ideology of Italian fascism change in the years 1919–22?

> (D) How far was the Italian Liberal state undermined in the years 1915–21?

Planning your answer

When you plan, organise your material in a way that will help you to answer the question.

For instance, for Question (C) you could begin by listing two or three ways in which Italian fascist ideology changed. Having done that, you could list two or three ways in which fascist ideology remained the same. Alternatively, you could arrange this information on one or two concept maps. Remember that your answer needs to be balanced. Therefore, it should provide points for and against change.

Each of these points will form the basis for one paragraph in your answer. In the last Skills Builder section, you considered the importance of providing specific examples to support your points. Don't forget this!

When you plan, there is no need to organise your material in a chronological way. This may encourage the writing of descriptive or narrative-style answers. Such answers may contain lots of accurate and relevant historical information, but may not be directly focused on the question.

Writing your answer

In Questions (C) and (D) you are asked 'how far' in relation to changes. So, in your final paragraph, the conclusion, you will be expected to *make a judgment*. Based on the historical evidence you have presented in your answer, you should decide, and state, whether you believe the situation mainly changed or stayed the same.

Activity: How much have you learned?

Here are some examples of questions which deal with causation and change. First, identify the causation questions and give a reason to support your choice. Then identify the questions which deal with change and give a reason for your choice. Finally, choose one 'causation' question and one 'change' question and produce a plan for each, showing how you would organise your answer.

> (E) How far was the 'mutilated victory' of the First World War the cause of instability in Italy between 1918 and 1922?

> (F) How far did economic conditions in Italy deteriorate between 1915 and 1921?

> (G) To what extent was fascist *squadrismo* responsible for Mussolini's appointment as prime minister in 1922?

> (H) How far did support for the Italian fascist movement change between 1919 and 1922?

Chapter 7 The Fascist consolidation and exercise of power 1922–43

Key questions

- How was a Fascist dictatorship established by 1925–26?
- How did the regime attempt to secure popular consent?
- What role did repression and terror play in Fascist Italy?

As the new prime minister, Mussolini was in a relatively weak position in October 1922. The PNF had only 35 deputies in the 535 member Chamber and just four ministers in the 14-strong Cabinet. By 1926, however, Mussolini had succeeded in creating his so-called 'regime of champions' – a personal dictatorship based on one-party rule. To generate popular support, the Fascist government launched a variety of propaganda initiatives ranging from indoctrination in schools to the establishment of a cult of personality which, at its height, gave the PNF leader an almost divine status. Repression and terror also formed part of the regime's strategy for staying in power, but the violence and coercion in Fascist Italy never reached the levels experienced in the Nazi and Soviet dictatorships.

Take note

As you read through this section, make notes to identify:

- the early measures Mussolini took to strengthen his position (1922–24)
- how Mussolini was able to survive the Matteotti crisis and cope with increasing pressure from the PNF radicals.

Timeline

November 1922	Mussolini granted emergency decree powers by the Chamber
December 1922	Fascist Grand Council established
January 1923	MVSN founded
July 1923	Acerbo Law passed
April 1924	Fascist bloc secured majority at general election
June 1924	PSU deputy Giacomo Matteotti murdered by Fascists
April 1925	OND founded
December 1925	Mussolini became head of government and *Duce*
January 1926	Head of government to make law by decree
April 1926	ONB founded
November 1926	Fascist one-party state created; OVRA and the 'Special Tribunal for the Defence of the State' established; 'anti-regime' publications banned
February 1929	Teachers compelled to take oath of loyalty
August 1931	Professors compelled to take oath of loyalty
June 1937	Anti-fascist Rosselli brothers murdered
1938–1939	Anti-Semitic legislation introduced; anti-Semitism taught in schools

Glossary

Coercion

Threats or force used to make somebody do something against his or her will.

The Fascist consolidation of power, 1922–26

Mussolini's early actions as prime minister

Without a Chamber majority, and unable to ignore parliament for fear of risking royal disapproval, Mussolini pursued a 'compromise and **coercion**' strategy to consolidate his power. A coalition with mainly liberal or PPI ministers reflected political reality and reassured conservative Italians.

The prime minister also made concessions to key institutions and groups such as the Catholic Church, the industrialists and the nationalists. From the outset, though, Mussolini strengthened his position by making himself interior minister and foreign minister. Furthermore, in November 1922, he used threats and assurances to obtain emergency decree powers (for 12 months) from the Chamber by 306 votes to 116. The Senate also gave its approval.

Mussolini began to exert greater personal authority over the Fascist Party too. In December 1922, he established a Fascist Grand Council of 22 prominent party members as the PNF's senior body and key policy-making forum. This marked an important step towards dictatorship. By controlling its membership and agenda, Mussolini could use the Grand Council to secure party approval for his major initiatives and control Fascist policy. Early in 1923, the squads were legalised and became the Voluntary Fascist Militia for National Security (MVSN). Bound by an oath of loyalty to Mussolini, the MVSN functioned as a state-funded full-time private army of 30,000 men. It also provided the *Duce* with a means of channelling the activism of **PNF intransigents** and reducing the influence of the provincial Fascist leaders.

The Acerbo Law, 1923

During June 1923, Under-secretary **Giacomo Acerbo** introduced a bill to permit the party that obtained the most votes in a general election to take two-thirds of the seats in the Chamber, provided it received 25% of the votes cast. The other parties would share the remaining seats on a proportional basis. Acerbo's reform, of course, was designed to secure a Fascist parliamentary majority: the militia and Fascist sympathisers in local government would ensure the 'right' poll result and Mussolini could order the police to ignore Fascist intimidation, violence and vote-rigging.

PNF 'intransigents' and 'revisionists'

The PNF was split into two basic groups. The larger 'intransigent' faction, including Roberto Farinacci, felt that Mussolini had betrayed the fascist revolution after the March on Rome with political compromises. They championed 'pure' *squadristi* fascism and demanded an immediate 'second wave' of the revolution to bring the state under complete PNF control. The smaller revisionist faction, including Dino Grandi, wanted to disarm the squads, end political violence and carry out a 'legal' and peaceful revolution. They advocated rule by a fascist elite (rather than PNF or parliamentary control).

Biography

Giacomo Acerbo

(1888–1969)

Leading Fascist minister and academic. After military service in the First World War Acerbo joined the PNF in August 1920 and was elected a deputy in 1921. He also helped to negotiate the Pact of Pacification with the socialists. Acerbo resigned as under-secretary after being accused of involvement in the murder of Giacomo Matteotti. He later returned as minister of agriculture and forests (1929–35). Although he opposed the regime's anti-Semitic policy in the late 1930s, he was eventually appointed minister of finance (1943). Acerbo voted against Mussolini in July 1943 and then resigned. After the war, he returned to university teaching.

In July 1923 the Chamber passed the Acerbo bill by 235 votes to 139. The menacing presence of Blackshirts during the debate certainly affected the outcome but the result was not simply due to intimidation. Most deputies believed that Mussolini was committed to parliamentary government and 'normalisation'. Other MPs either applauded the government's anti-left-wing line or saw electoral reform as the way to avoid weak coalition ministries.

Giacomo Matteotti

(1885–1924)

Arguably the most able socialist of his generation, Matteotti opposed Italy's entry into the First World War and was elected as a deputy in 1919. In the early 1920s, he was physically attacked on several occasions by fascists. He called for a united front against the PNF and brought the violent nature of fascism to international attention. In October 1922 he left the PSI, later becoming the general secretary of the PSU. After his death, Matteotti became an anti-fascist martyr within and outside Italy.

Matteotti is remembered by the PSI, 1947

Mussolini held a general election under the new Acerbo system in April 1924. The PNF formed an electoral alliance with right-wing liberals including Salandra, and received support from Giolitti's faction. On a two-thirds turnout (7.6 million Italians), the Fascist bloc obtained 65% of the vote and 374 of the 535 seats. This resounding victory reflected Mussolini's growing popularity but widespread Blackshirt violence and ballot rigging also influenced the result. Nevertheless, despite Fascist intimidation, the opposition parties – including the PSI, PSU, PCI and the PPI – still received 2.5 million votes overall.

The Matteotti crisis, 1924

When parliament reconvened, opposition deputies denounced the Fascist violence and ballot rigging at the recent election. Mussolini's most outspoken critic was the anti-Fascist PSU MP, **Giacomo Matteotti**. On 30 May 1924, amid Fascist heckling in the Chamber, Matteotti condemned Blackshirt illegality at the polls. Eleven days later, Fascists led by Amerigo Dumini abducted and killed Matteotti. His body was discovered outside Rome in August. Dumini, an assistant to the prime minister's press secretary, Cesare Rossi, was part of Mussolini's entourage and ran his secret hit squad, the *Cheka*. Even if he had not ordered the killing, Mussolini was politically and morally responsible for Matteotti's death. He had established the *Cheka* and had previously ordered attacks on opponents. Shortly before the murder, Mussolini had also expressed his loathing of Matteotti and this would have encouraged the PNF radicals to act. Matteotti's death caused widespread anger and dismay in Italy.

Mussolini's political survival depended on the response of the establishment, the parliamentary opposition and the PNF intransigents. The establishment generally overlooked the Matteotti affair because they saw no acceptable alternative to Mussolini. Victor Emmanuel feared that Mussolini's dismissal, soon after securing a parliamentary majority, would strengthen the revolutionary Left and trigger a civil war. The Senate, a crucial barometer of elite opinion, endorsed ongoing government 'pacification' measures by 225 votes to 21 in late June. Senior army officers registered their support by donating over 100,000 surplus rifles to the MVSN and the Vatican journal *Osservatore Romano* also backed Mussolini. Furthermore, most industrialists accepted politics was often a brutal business and preferred to focus on their profits.

Mussolini prudently made concessions and reshuffled his government to cement establishment support. He publically deplored Matteotti's murder, sacked several leading Fascists (including De Bono – see page 57 – and Rossi) and brought in people acceptable to the elite, notably the nationalist journalist Luigi Federzoni, who became minister of the interior. The *Cheka* was dissolved and the militia had to swear allegiance to the king. In addition, four prominent Fascists – Dumini, Rossi, Filippo Filippelli and Giovanni Marinelli – were arrested in connection with Matteotti's death.

In protest at the murder, opposition deputies (mainly Socialists, Communists and PPI dissidents) abandoned the Chamber and set up their own assembly. The PNF also faced a hostile press campaign. Yet the parliamentary opposition's protest strengthened Mussolini too. Their walk-out merely turned the Chamber into a compliant pro-government body and provided Victor Emmanuel with an excuse to do nothing. In any case, divisions soon resurfaced between the Socialists, Communists, opposition liberals and Catholics, which made a united anti-fascist front impossible.

Matteotti's murder also brought the tensions between the PNF leader and the intransigents to a head. Party radicals resented government 'normalisation', the anti-fascist press campaign and the appointment of non-Fascist ministers. They wanted to start the next phase of the revolution. On 31 December 1924, 10,000 armed Blackshirts rioted in Florence, destroying opposition party headquarters and newspaper offices. To reinforce the point, 33 militia leaders confronted Mussolini and demanded an immediate fascist revolution. He now faced a major crisis: the intransigents were on the verge of rebellion but an actual fascist rising would probably alienate the king and prompt military action against the PNF. Forced into a corner, Mussolini decided to pre-empt the radicals by introducing his own 'second wave' – and seizing power.

Creating the Fascist dictatorship, 1925–26

In a crucial speech to the Chamber on 3 January 1925, Mussolini posed as the responsible statesman. Denying any direct involvement in Matteotti's death, he emphasised his government's commitment to 'normalisation' and legal methods. Nevertheless, he accepted sole 'political, moral and historical responsibility for all that has happened' and declared that 'if fascism has been a criminal association, then I am the chief of this criminal association'. He railed against the opposition for leaving parliament and condemned the press campaign against the government. Italy, he concluded, required a stronger regime to deal with political opponents and remove the need to unleash the fascist squads. This skilful speech extricated Mussolini from a difficult position. Fascist radicals, encouraged by his defence of fascism, assumed that, in future, the government would listen to their views. Most of the establishment were reassured too and continued to back Mussolini. They were relieved that the squads would not be used and that state agencies such as the police and the prefects would restore law and order. By taking the initiative, Mussolini was now able to take firm action against the political opposition.

After making this speech, Mussolini closed down some 400 'suspect' organisations, confiscated all illegally held weapons and had about 100 'subversives' arrested. The remaining non-fascist ministers resigned and Liberal Italy's elder statesmen – Giolitti, Orlando and Salandra – joined the parliamentary opposition.

Over the next two years, Mussolini created a personal dictatorship which developed in a piecemeal and improvised way. Several factors enabled the PNF leader to establish one-man rule.

Matteotti murder trial, 1925

In November 1925, Rossi and Marinelli were found guilty of organising an act of violence against Matteotti, but not murder. Eventually, the five Fascists involved in the actual abduction were put on trial in March 1926. Three of them, including Dumini, were found guilty of unpremeditated murder. They were each sentenced to six years in prison but were released after just two months. The other two defendants were acquitted.

Take note

As you read through this section, make notes to identify the measures introduced in 1925–26 which transformed Italy into a Fascist dictatorship. How do they differ from the early years of Mussolini's rule?

Take note

As you read through this section, make bullet-point notes on the main ways in which the regime used the following means to generate support for fascism:
• the education system
• Fascist organisations
• the Italian media.
How successful were Fascist indoctrination and propaganda methods?

- First, by July 1925, the government was exclusively Fascist and could now pursue its objectives with fewer internal constraints.

- Second, the Fascist-dominated Chamber (which had been made more manageable by the walk-out of opposition deputies) compliantly rubber-stamped the repressive decrees that built Mussolini's authoritarian system.

- Third, the government tightened press censorship immediately after the 3 January speech to deprive the anti-fascist parties of their main political weapon.

- Finally, four unsuccessful **assassination attempts** on Mussolini between November 1925 and October 1926 alarmed the king and ordinary Italians, and were used as a pretext to entrench Mussolini's power, undermine opponents and increase repression.

In the three months following the first attempt, in November 1925, several draconian laws were passed which banned secret organisations (including freemasonry), made 'anti-government' conduct by public employees a sackable offence and established an official register of approved journalists. Another measure, aimed at the 10,000 anti-fascist exiles, permitted the authorities to cancel the citizenship and confiscate the property of any Italian living abroad who 'damaged' Italian interests.

Two constitutional amendments also reinforced Mussolini's position. The first (December 1925) changed his official title to Head of the Government and *Duce*, and abolished parliament's right to remove the prime minister with a no confidence vote. The second (January 1926) allowed the head of the government to make law by decree. Mussolini could now circumvent parliament altogether. Other repressive measures followed. Political organisations and publications found guilty of 'actions against the regime' were banned, which effectively established a one-party state with a Fascist controlled press. Capital punishment was introduced for the attempted assassination of the royal family and the head of the government. The Chamber also excluded the walk-out deputies permanently and banned the PCI. Widely criticised for failing to protect the *Duce*, the interior minister, Federzoni, was removed too. Mussolini took over his post.

Winning hearts and minds for the Fascist regime

Fascism and education

Once in power, Mussolini's government launched various initiatives and organisations to secure popular support for Fascist rule. The regime's growing control over schools and universities was an important aspect of this drive to instil fascist values. In December 1925, Mussolini instructed schools to educate young Italians to live according to the fascist revolution. His directive was followed by an official purge of 'politically incompatible' teachers. From 1929, primary and secondary school teachers had to take an oath of loyalty to the regime and, by 1933, PNF membership was a condition of employment. A year later, primary school staff were ordered to wear Blackshirt uniforms in the classroom.

The school curriculum also became more ideological from the mid-1920s. After banning almost one-third of the history books used in schools in 1926, the government introduced a single primary textbook in 1928 covering all subjects in an approved manner to encourage conformity. Lessons increasingly celebrated the *Duce*, militarism and imperialism. Furthermore, the school curriculum was adapted to reflect the regime's shifting priorities. Religious instruction was made compulsory in all secondary schools after Mussolini's 1929 Concordat with the Vatican (see Chapter 8), and, as the Fascist system became overtly racist in the late 1930s, primary textbooks emphasised Italy's 'civilising mission'. In 1939, **Guiseppe Bottai**, the education minister, introduced a **School Charter** which was designed to create the new 'fascist man'. Due to the outbreak of the Second World War, however, little came of Bottai's plan.

Even though an increasing number of young Italians were educated under the Fascist regime, their efforts to influence school pupils were only partially successful. Many teachers who survived the purge of the profession remained committed to other political beliefs. They simply accommodated themselves to the regime to safeguard their own interests. Regular ministerial orders and instructions caused much resentment among staff in Italian schools and, as a result, official directives were often carried out with little enthusiasm in the classroom. In rural communities, inadequate teaching resources coupled with high levels of absenteeism and illiteracy due to children undertaking agricultural work, particularly at harvest time, also limited the impact of Fascist educational policy. Over one-fifth of brides in southern Italy in 1936 could not sign the marriage register.

During the 1930s the government focused on the universities as well. In 1930 the regime required all rectors and deans to have been PNF members for at least five years and, in 1931, university professors were obliged to take an oath of loyalty to the Fascist state. Just 11 out of 1250 academics declined. Many took the oath to prevent Fascist appointees taking over university posts but the small number of refusals gave Mussolini a propaganda coup. From 1933, all new professors had to be party members. Generally speaking though, the universities were not harassed provided they did not engage in anti-Fascist political activity. Indeed, by the late 1930s, many undergraduates were favourably disposed to the regime because they had been indoctrinated to some extent by the school system and the Fascist youth organisation.

Fascism and youth

The *Opera Nazionale Balilla* (*Balilla* or ONB) – the Fascist youth movement – also helped to inculcate fascist values. With its slogan 'Believe, Obey, Fight', the ONB had been established in 1926 by the Ministry of Education to turn young Italians aged between six and 18 into fascists. Within a year, it had 1,236,000 members.

Biography

Guiseppe Bottai

(1895–1959)

Leading Fascist revisionist and journalist. A futurist and former *Arditi* commando, Bottai helped to establish the fascist movement in Rome and was elected a deputy in 1921. He also launched the journal *Critica Fascista* (1923–43) which argued for revisionist fascism. As minister of corporations (1926–32), he attempted to make the corporate state function effectively but was thwarted by Mussolini's indifference and industrialists' hostility. He opposed Mussolini at the July 1943 Fascist Grand Council meeting and left Italy later that year. He returned in 1948 to resume his journalistic career.

School Charter, 1939

This programme aimed to (a) strengthen PNF-school links, (b) remove class barriers in education, (c) raise the profile of science and technology, (d) establish special schools for rural children and (e) make manual work part of the overall curriculum.

School	1923	1936
Primary	3.98m	5.19m
Secondary	326,604	674,546

Pupils in Italian schools under the Fascist regime

Balilla youth clubs offered sport, summer camps and pre-military training. Italian youths were probably more attracted by the facilities than the propaganda message but the *Balilla* certainly boosted the regime. Once under party control in 1937, it was renamed the GIL (*Gioventú Italiana del Littorio*) and membership became compulsory two years later. At that point, the GIL had almost 7.9 million members.

The GUF (*Gioventú Universitaria Fascista*) was a similar organisation for university students which ran popular athletic and debating competitions. Most joined for social or career reasons and the regime tolerated a certain amount of dissent and criticism within the GUF because it was created to help nurture and select the next generation of the Fascist elite.

The *Opera Nazionale Dopolavoro*

The Fascist organisation which did most to foster public identification with the regime was the *Opera Nazionale Dopolavoro* (*Dopolavoro* or OND), a national network of subsidised Fascist leisure clubs for public- and private-sector workers. Formed in 1925 and expanded under party control from 1927, the OND provided sport, music, films, plays, dancing, organised holidays and excursions to the coast. It also provided welfare for poor families. At its height, the *Dopolavoro* ran over 11,000 sports clubs and by 1935 controlled 771 cinemas, 2066 theatre companies, 2130 orchestras and 6427 libraries. Although membership was not compulsory, it became the largest and most active adult organisation. In 1939 some 4 million Italians belonged to the OND. Manual and non-manual workers joined but they tended to stick with their own class when participating in OND activities. With its emphasis on leisure activities rather than overt indoctrination, the *Dopolavoro* was a genuinely popular innovation which encouraged general acceptance of fascism. The function and informal class segregation of the OND, however, meant it could neither instil fascism's militaristic values nor foster a real sense of national community.

The Cult of the *Duce*

Mussolini was a brilliant tactician and opportunist who understood better than his rivals how Italian politics had changed after the First World War. His skill at political manoeuvring was partly due to a lack of firmly held ethical and ideological beliefs. Consequently, he used institutions and individuals for as long as they served his interests. Mussolini's short-term political shrewdness was matched by an ability to communicate effectively through public speeches and the newspapers. Throughout his political career, however, he remained an insecure and impressionable man who suffered from an inferiority complex. His outward displays of self-confidence and assertiveness were undoubtedly a form of compensation for his inner sense of inadequacy. Mussolini the man could never live up to the propaganda image of the *Duce*.

Mussolini in 1923, acclaimed as the 'Theodore Roosevelt' of Italy, during a visit of the British royal family

At the centre of the regime's efforts to generate popular support was the cult of the *Duce* (or *ducismo*) which depicted Mussolini as Italy's saviour. Posters, films, newspapers, biographies and official statements all conveyed an image of super-human intellectual, physical and sporting abilities. At its peak in the 1930s, *ducismo* accorded Mussolini semi-divine status and created the myth of the omnipotent and omniscient leader. His supposed infallibility led to the slogan 'Mussolini is always right', which became a mantra for the regime. All this fed the *Duce*'s vanity but it was politically useful too. The cult of the leader elevated him above, and set him apart from, the Fascist system.

This brought Mussolini two benefits: his personal prestige helped to sustain the regime and any problems could be blamed on other Fascists or the government, not him. Indeed, *ducismo* became the main unifying force in Fascist Italy, because Mussolini's personal popularity (which dipped only briefly in the early 1930s due to the economic downturn and disagreements with the pope) generally remained very high until the Second World War. Outwardly at least, he came almost to accept the cult as proof of his political genius and indispensability. He even had to be consulted about the date when Rome's traffic police could switch to their summer uniforms!

Control of the press

As a journalist and editor, Mussolini knew that a Fascist-controlled press could mobilise public support for the regime. By 1926, all opposition newspapers had been closed down and other publications, either through conviction or coercion, had decided to toe the Fascist line. The dictatorship also ran its own official news agency and only government-registered journalists were allowed to write. Newspapers were expected to give minimal coverage to sensitive topics such as crime and unemployment. Fines were imposed for non-compliance, though most editors censored their own publications. Mussolini also contacted editors and newspaper owners privately to ensure that the 'right' events were reported in the appropriate way. From 1934, the regime tightened press instructions about what to cover and how to depict the dictator. Three years later, a Ministry of Popular Culture assumed control of the newspapers and other media, including radio and the cinema, in a continuing drive to convert the masses to fascism.

Yet the state's attempts to use the press as a propaganda outlet were not that successful. Fascist newspapers accounted for just 10% of total circulation and some local Fascist publications openly criticised the regime for its lack of radicalism. Other journals found ways of discussing controversial topics such as the pros and cons of a settlement with the papacy in 1929. It also proved impossible to stamp out the underground anti-fascist press. Italians had access to other sources of information as well, namely the foreign media (newspapers and radio programmes) and tourists. The Fascist press campaign was further hindered by the fact that sections of the population remained functionally illiterate.

The cult of the *Duce*

Under *ducismo*, the worship of Mussolini reached extraordinary heights:

- By the early 1930s, some 30 million publicity pictures of the dictator were in general circulation in Italy.
- Fascist propaganda claimed he was the 'greatest Italian in history' and the nation's 'first sportsman'.
- Fascist sources also maintained that he worked 20 hours a day in the service of his country (in reality he went to bed early each night).
- A mountain and a black rose were even renamed in his honour!

Mussolini, as depicted in the newspaper *La Domenica del Corriere* in 1930

Radio and cinema

After 1924, the regime also used the expanding state-controlled radio network to put its political message across through a diet of music, drama, official broadcasts and live speeches from Mussolini. By 1938 about 1 million Italians possessed a radio, which meant that about 5 million listened to a privately owned set. Many more listened in public, partly because the government supplied schools with radios and the OND held group 'listening' meetings. These initiatives helped the Fascists target rural areas and the illiterate.

To some extent, cinema – the most popular form of entertainment in Italy in the 1930s – served the same purpose. From 1924 a government agency, LUCE, produced documentaries and newsreels with some political content which, by law, had to be shown to audiences before the main film. Imported and Italian films were censored by the state, which set out strict guidelines on style and content. A few Italian feature films, including *Luciano Serra, pilota*, (which charted the life of an Italian airman in the Abyssinian war) praised fascism and its achievements. Most films, however, were escapist or historical dramas, and the overwhelming majority of Italian cinema-goers preferred them to explicit Fascist propaganda. In 1938, US films accounted for about 75% of Italian cinema ticket sales. The most popular feature was *Snow White and the Seven Dwarfs*. Thus, although Mussolini saw the cinema as 'the strongest weapon', it had a limited propaganda impact on the Italian population.

Repression and terror under the Fascist regime

The OVRA

Repression and terror, of course, were also key elements of the regime and tightened Mussolini's grip on power. In November 1926 a new secret police force, **OVRA**, was created under **Arturo Bocchini**, who declared that fascism was to exert 'a constant but not too conspicuous oppression'. Initially, OVRA was set up to investigate and combat anti-fascist activity but increasingly gathered information, and reported, on all aspects of Italian life. The organisation compiled files on 130,000 potential 'subversives', established a network of some 100,000 informants and, by 1930, organised some 20,000 raids each week. However, with only a relatively small full-time staff (around 700 agents in the 1930s), and run by career officials rather than Fascist ideologues, Mussolini's secret police never rivalled Hitler's *Gestapo* or Stalin's NKVD for repression.

Biography

Arturo Bocchini

(1880–1940)

A career civil servant who joined the Ministry of the Interior in 1903, Bocchini became the prefect of Genoa (1925) and was then appointed chief of police by the *Duce* in 1926. Known as the 'Shield of Mussolini', he was personally loyal to the dictator but also protected the police from PNF control. Bocchini effectively destroyed the PCI and helped to control the Fascist intransigents too. Lacking any firm fascist convictions, he disapproved of the anti-Semitic legislation of the late 1930s and opposed Italy's entry into the Second World War. Bocchini remained head of the police and OVRA until his death.

Bocchini (right) with Heinrich Himmler, 1938

OVRA detained some 6000 political opponents (mainly communists or members of the non-party anti-fascist revolutionary movement, **Justice and Liberty**) between 1930 and 1934 – an average of 125 each month – but few of them ended up in gaol. On Mussolini's orders, OVRA even spied on senior Fascists Balbo and Farinacci, who subsequently found out that they had been placed under surveillance. Both men complained but the *Duce* ignored their protests.

Another instrument of coercion was the MVSN, the armed Fascist militia, which was used to intimidate opponents.

The Special Tribunal and *Confino*

A 'Special Tribunal for the Defence of the State', operating under martial law, was also introduced in November 1926 to tackle serious political dissent. Between 1927 and 1943, the Tribunal tried some 21,000 people and imposed gaol terms averaging five years in 5100 cases. The most prominent victim was the Communist leader Antonio Gramsci, who was given a 20-year prison sentence. It also condemned 49 people to death. During the 1930s, the Special Tribunal imprisoned up to 365 anti-fascists annually.

From late 1926, political prisoners could also be sent into internal exile (*confino*) in remote provinces or penal colonies located on islands off the mainland, such as Lipari. Some Italians were banished in this way for five years simply because the authorities suspected that they were contemplating action against the regime. *Confino* was spartan, and sometimes brutal, but internal exiles were not compelled to work, received a 10 lire daily allowance and could take their families with them. By 1943, about 14,000 people had been 'confined' at some stage under Fascist rule.

Many prominent opponents fled abroad, either to avoid Blackshirt persecution or to protest against the regime. These exiles included the ex-prime minister Nitti, the socialist leader Filippo Turati and the PPI leader Luigi Sturzo. Mussolini denounced those who left Italy as 'outsiders' and Fascist agents tracked down a number of them, such as the **Rosselli brothers**, and murdered them.

Evidence of Fascist repression was everywhere. The press and parliament were essentially powerless, telephone calls and the post were monitored, and Italian society was riddled with police informers. At local level, petty-minded and sometimes vicious Fascist officials ruled through intimidation and used their positions to settle personal and political scores. Nevertheless, these repressive features did not stifle traditional forms of protest such as land occupations, food price riots and strikes over pay and conditions. Anti-fascist humour and graffiti were also widespread. Most Italians adopted *afascismo* – an attitude of passive acceptance or lukewarm conformity – because there appeared to be no alternative to Mussolini's government. Fascism was generally tolerated and the dissent that existed posed no real threat to the regime. Still, it was telling that the *Duce* would neither allow free speech nor disband the militia.

Justice and Liberty

Founded in 1929 as an activist anti-fascist organisation, Justice and Liberty appealed to young intellectuals, democrats, republicans and socialists. It developed an underground network and, by the early 1930s, probably rivalled the PCI in terms of support.

Biography

Rosselli brothers

Carlo (1899–1937)
Nello (1900–1937)

The Rosselli brothers were co-founders of Justice and Liberty and well-known opponents of Mussolini's regime. Born into a wealthy Tuscan Jewish family, both were reformist socialists and belonged to the PSU. After helping Turati flee to France, Carlo was arrested by the Fascist authorities but escaped to Paris in 1929. Later he fought as a volunteer on the Republican side in the Spanish Civil War and wrote a book entitled *Liberal Socialism*, which rejected communism in favour of moderate left-wing politics. Nello joined his brother in exile and was also involved in socialist and anti-fascist activities abroad. They were killed in the French town of Bagnoles-de-l'Orne in June 1937 by French fascists acting on the Italian government's orders.

The anti-Semitic decrees of 1938–39

Anti-Semitism (hostility and discrimination against Jews) was a central element in Nazi ideology and led to the systematic persecution of Jews under the Third Reich. These laws, which were never popular in Italy, imposed the following restrictions:

- Foreign Jews were to be deported.
- Italian Jews could not marry 'Aryan' (Hitler's 'master race') Italians.
- Jews were banned from state employment, the PNF and the armed forces.
- Jewish children could not attend state schools.
- Jews could not own more than 50 hectares of land or run a business with over 100 employees.
- Jews could not enter professions such as journalism and law.

Italian fascism and anti-Semitism

Before 1938, anti-Semitism had not been an official feature of the Italian Fascist regime. Mussolini rejected Nazi racial doctrine, appointed Guido Jung, a Jew, as finance minister (1932–35) and had a Jewish mistress, Margherita Sarfatti. Indeed, over 10,000 Jews belonged to the PNF by 1938. Moreover, the 50,000 Jews living in Italy could not be perceived as a threat or problem because they accounted for just 0.1 per cent of the population. Having said this, some Fascists (such as Farinacci) were anti-Semitic and the *Duce* occasionally criticised the Jews for their beliefs or actions.

In the late 1930s, however, as Mussolini's Italy built closer ties with Hitler's Germany, the Fascist government launched an anti-Semitic campaign which was designed to remove the Jews from Italian life. Several **anti-Semitic decrees** were introduced between September 1938 and June 1939, which imposed a variety of restrictions on the Jewish community. As a result of these measures, some 7000 Jews were forced out of the armed services, 181 Jewish teachers and academics were sacked, 400 Jewish state employees lost their jobs, and 5600 Jewish students were expelled from schools and universities.

Over the next three years, around 6000 Italian Jews emigrated. Many Jewish-owned businesses closed down too. Once Italy had entered the Second World War on the side of Germany in 1940, all foreign Jews were interned and several thousand were sent to a concentration camp in Calabria. Italian Jews were conscripted by the government to perform heavy manual tasks.

The anti-Semitic laws of 1938–39 were introduced due to:

- Mussolini's desire to express solidarity with his ally, Nazi Germany
- a hardening of racist and imperialist attitudes following the conquest of Abyssinia
- Jewish opposition (e.g. the Rosselli brothers) to the regime
- the drive to radicalise and galvanise Fascist Italy during the 1930s in preparation for war.

Conclusion: Consent or coercion?

Mussolini once famously claimed that the domestic opposition to his regime was limited to just 2000 individuals. This did not mean, however, that the overwhelming majority of Italians supported the Fascist dictatorship. Certainly, as we have seen, the cult of the *Duce* and organisations such as the OND helped the regime to achieve a level of popularity and public consent. It is also true that young Italians growing up in the Fascist education and youth systems after 1925 were more susceptible to propaganda and indoctrination. They had no experience of pre-Fascist Italy and their lives were now regimented by Mussolini's government. Yet all of these support-building measures and organisations operated in a climate of state repression and coercion which would not allow people to express their views freely and pressured them into activities backed by the regime. Understandably, most Italians had no wish to be arrested by the OVRA, sent before the Special Tribunal or confined, so they conformed rather than actively consented. In this fundamental sense, therefore, coercion was the key element that maintained fascist rule.

Activity: Consent or coercion?

1. In a word-processing document, draw a table with four columns and nine rows. Label the columns: Measure; Successes; Failures; Consent or coercion? In the first column, labelled 'Measure', add each of the following on a separate row: education; ONB; OND; the cult of the *Duce*; the press; radio and cinema; OVRA; the Special Tribunal and *confino*; anti-Semitic measures.

2. Use the information in this chapter and from other sources to complete the table, noting down the successes and failures of each measure, and deciding whether it was part of a move to build consent or whether it was coercion.

3. Once you have completed the table, use your findings to:

    (a) place the Fascist methods in order of effectiveness

    (b) write a short report (about one side of A4 paper) to make the case for either consent or coercion as the most important factor in maintaining Fascist rule.

Taking it further

Search the internet for propaganda images of Mussolini (try typing 'Mussolini' or 'cult of the Duce' into a search engine image search). These could be posters, photographs or other images. You could start with http://casahistoria.net/Fascism.html but there are several other good websites. Choose five contrasting images. Print these out or import them into an electronic document. Make notes around the images to highlight the key features of the cult of the *Duce* (mentioned above). Try to remember these images when you are revising for your exam – they could be useful examples for your essays!

Chapter 8: **The Fascist state: 1925–43**

Key questions

- How did the Fascist regime manage the Italian economy?
- Did conditions improve for the citizens of Italy?
- What was the relationship between the Fascist state and the groups within it?
- What was the significance of the Lateran Pacts with the Catholic Church?

The *Duce* had no real knowledge of, or interest in, economics. In fact, he came to power without any detailed plans for industry and agriculture. He did understand, however, that only a strong economy could deliver his key objectives – a secure personal dictatorship, increased military strength and an Italian empire. Mussolini also knew that his regime could function properly only with the support of influential groups and institutions in Italian society. For this reason, the *Duce*'s government went to considerable lengths to incorporate them within the Fascist system. The formal reconciliation with the Vatican in 1929 provided another important source of political stability and resolved long-standing problems in the relationship between the Italian state and the Catholic Church.

Take note

As you read through this section:

- identify why and how Fascist economic policy changed 1922–29
- assess the value of the Corporate State for the regime
- list the key measures introduced by the regime to tackle the Depression
- identify the successes and failures of the Fascist economy up to 1939
- assess the strength of the Italian wartime economy.

Glossary

Liberal economic policies

Such policies promote the free market, the private sector, free trade between nations and limited government involvement in the economy.

Timeline

1923	PNF merger with the Italian Nationalist Association
1925	Battle for Grain launched; Vidoni Pact between *Confindustria* and Fascist syndicates
1926	Rocco Law passed; Ministry of Corporations established
1927	'Quota 90' and Battle for Births launched; Ruralisation campaign started; Labour Charter introduced
1928	'Mussolini Law' on land reclamation introduced; Electoral law
1929	Lateran Pacts between the Fascist state and the Catholic Church
1931/33	IMI and IRI founded
1936	Bank of Italy nationalised
1939	Chamber of Deputies replaced with the Chamber of Fasces and Corporations
1943	Large-scale industrial strikes in Piedmont and Lombardy

Fascism and the economy

Mussolini's economic policy, 1922–29

In his first years as prime minister, Mussolini pursued **liberal economic policies** which pleased many industrialists. He appointed Alberto De Stefani – an economics professor and former First World War soldier – as his finance minister and introduced various pro-business measures. Taxes on war profits were reduced or abolished, private companies took over the telephone system and Ansaldo (the large shipping and steel firm) received a cash injection from the state. These early years coincided with a general European economic recovery and the decline of the Italian Left, both of which strengthened business confidence. Consequently, from 1921–25, manufacturing output in Italy increased by almost 54% and a budget surplus was produced in 1924.

The boom years ended in 1925–26 due to rising **inflation**, a trade deficit crisis and the falling value of the lira. These problems, and the creation of the Fascist dictatorship, led to a shift in economic policy. Mussolini replaced De Stefani with a new finance minister, the banker and industrialist Count Giuseppe Volpi, in 1925. Unlike De Stefani, Volpi backed government loans to industry, state intervention, high tariffs and a balanced budget. His appointment was a clear sign that Mussolini wanted good relations with big business. Volpi pursued **deflationary and protectionist policies**, which set the tone for the rest of the Fascist era.

In 1926, for reasons of national and personal prestige, the *Duce* insisted that the lira (then at 150 to the pound sterling) was undervalued and should be reset at 90 lira to the British pound. 'Quota 90' was put into effect the following year. Foreign financiers and the Italian public applauded Mussolini's decision but it had a damaging impact on the economy. The high cost of the lira meant that Italian goods almost doubled in price abroad and Italian export industries, notably textiles, light engineering and car manufacturing, suffered. Between 1922 and 1926, Italy's economic boom had been largely export-led. Moreover, imported foods and products did not become more affordable through revaluation because the regime imposed higher tariffs on some foreign goods and enforced 10% pay cuts. These wage reductions were part of the regime's deflationary policy. Only industries which required large supplies of cheap tariff-free raw materials from abroad and which relied mainly on domestic orders, really benefited from 'Quota 90' and a protected home market.

By 1929, 'the Fascist economic pattern was becoming set. Italy was turning away from her export markets, and boosting instead the industries which stood to gain most from empire and rearmament.' (Martin Clark, 2008)

The Corporate State

In the mid-1920s, production was officially reorganised under the **Corporate State**, the much-heralded Fascist 'third way' between capitalism and communism. Fascist propaganda claimed this new mechanism would end class conflict and promote social harmony by incorporating both bosses and workers inside the state. Mussolini also believed that corporate economics would support an expansionist foreign policy. Under the Vidoni Pact of 1925, *Confindustria* (the Italian Industrialists' Confederation) and the Fascist syndicates (trade unions) recognised each other as the exclusive representatives respectively of capital and labour, but the regime was not even-handed. The 1926 Rocco Law and the 1927 Labour Charter placed the Fascist unions under state control and created a labour relations system which favoured employers. Furthermore, in 1928, the Confederation of Fascist Syndicates was split into six sections. This ensured that the Fascist unions were susceptible to greater state control and posed little threat either to the government or to the industrialists' aims.

Glossary

Inflation

Inflation occurs when the amount of money and credit in an economy increases relative to the supply of goods and services, and this leads to rising prices.

Deflationary and protectionist policies

Deflationary policies usually cut government spending, increase taxes, restrict imports and reduce wages to balance the national budget and stop inflation. Protectionist policies are designed to protect home industries from foreign competition using tariffs or import duties, or import quotas placing formal limits on foreign goods entering the country.

Glossary

The Corporate State

Designed to place employers and workers under direct state control to ensure national needs took priority over sectional interests. In theory, corporatism was decentralised but, in reality, the regime controlled policy, and government appointees and employers dominated decision-making within the corporations.

The Corporate State extended Fascist control but failed to deliver greater economic efficiency due to widespread corruption, administrative confusion and wasteful practices. It also created a vast bureaucracy which proved a serious economic burden. In 1939, corporatism became the basis of Italian political life when the Chamber of Deputies was replaced with a Chamber of Fasces and Corporations.

Gold standard

A financial mechanism designed to give a currency strength and stability by allowing banknotes to be converted into or out of gold.

IMI

The Institute for Italian Securities was a state-funded rescue agency which bought worthless company shares from the banks and provided long-term loans to industry.

IRI

The Institute for Industrial Reconstruction intervened to save a range of enterprises and played a central role in extending state control over sectors of the Italian economy.

To give this 'third way' some credibility, a Ministry of Corporations was set up in 1926 and, over the next 12 years, a Corporate State of sorts was fitfully developed. In fact, the project never really got off the ground. Controlled by party bosses, the corporations developed into a vast, lumbering, centralised bureaucracy with an interventionist culture that discouraged industrial innovation and efficiency. The *Duce* undoubtedly recognised the propaganda value of the Corporate State but never took corporatism that seriously. There was no 'Battle for the Corporations', the regime did not use the Corporate State to tackle the Depression, and the system was introduced in a piecemeal fashion. Mussolini also knew he had to be cautious rather than radical because he could not afford to alienate Italy's economic elite. Stripped of its 'third-way' mask, the Corporate State institutionalised workplace exploitation and served the regime and the employers' interests.

The Great Depression

In 1929 a major depression hit the US economy then spread to all the capitalist nations in Europe. It reduced international trade sharply and created mass unemployment in the countries concerned.

Fascist Italy weathered this Great Depression, which lasted until 1936, relatively well. The economy was not heavily dependent on world markets and had a limited industrial sector. Imports and consumption had already been cut, and high import tariffs and exchange controls gave some protection from foreign recession. Nevertheless, the economic downturn did have an impact. Between 1929 and 1933, industrial production fell by 23% and unemployment increased from 300,000 to 1.3 million. By 1936, exports and imports had dropped by one-third. Those still in work in the early 1930s faced wage cuts – state employees and farm workers had their pay reduced by 12 and 25% respectively. Furthermore, Mussolini's decision to stay on the **gold standard** until 1936 had a negative effect because it overvalued the currency at about 60 lire to the British pound.

To tackle these problems, the regime introduced public works schemes and increased government expenditure and state intervention. Spending on employment-creation schemes tripled between 1929 and 1934, resulting in some 240,000 new state jobs through road construction, marsh drainage and government bureaucracy. A piecemeal Fascist 'welfare state' was also established. Pensions, sick pay, paid holidays and unemployment benefit were all introduced by 1933 and, within six years, almost 30% of the population belonged to the state health insurance scheme. In the late 1930s, social security spending accounted for 21% of total state expenditure.

The government also had to intervene to save the banks, as hard-pressed companies defaulted on their loans. Mussolini introduced the state-funded **IMI** in 1931 to take over the banks' role of granting long-term industrial loans. Two years later, another agency – the **IRI**, was set up to help struggling businesses and banks. By purchasing the banks' shares in failing enterprises, the IRI helped to prevent financial collapse and came to own large sectors of the economy. In 1936 the Bank of Italy was nationalised.

By 1939 the IRI controlled 90% of shipbuilding, 75% of pig iron and 45% of steel production. Public bodies and agencies were also established to run other parts of the economy using industrialists and businessmen from the relevant sectors. In Europe, only the Soviet Union had a larger proportion of its economy under state control. This broad policy of state intervention was driven more by pragmatism than ideology, yet it still had a significant effect. By 1939 the Fascist state controlled over 20% of Italian industry.

The drive for autarky

In 1935, Mussolini invaded Abyssinia (see Chapter 10). As a consequence, the League of Nations imposed economic sanctions on Italy and this accelerated the regime's pursuit of **autarky**. The *Duce* concluded that this would mark Italy out as a great independent nation. He also reasoned that, as a major war was virtually inevitable, the economy had to be able to produce all the resources required for Italy to win a modern conflict. **Ersatz goods** were developed to replace imports; tariffs and import quotas were introduced; and state agencies such as AGIP (an oil company) searched for new energy sources. In addition, large government contracts were given to the steel, chemical and shipbuilding industries and state control over the economy was increased.

To boost output further, major companies were permitted to merge into virtual monopolies or **cartels**. Under these arrangements, for example, FIAT controlled car manufacturing and Montecatini and SNIA Viscosa dominated chemical production. Nevertheless, by 1940, the Italian economy faced major problems. The huge cost of rearmament and the Fascist military interventions in Abyssinia and Spain had increased Italy's budget deficit from 2 billion to 28 billion lire between 1934 and 1939, despite higher taxes. Mussolini's focus on heavy industry to secure his foreign policy objectives had also distorted the development of the Italian economy. Export industries were largely neglected and the state opted for the products of high-cost domestic industries rather than buying the same items more cheaply from abroad.

The Battle for Births

The regime's preoccupation with autarky, military strength and imperial expansion was also clearly reflected in the **Battle for Births**, which began in 1927. Mussolini wanted the population to rise to 60 million Italians by 1950 (from 41 million in 1931) so the nation would have enough soldiers to win a modern war and enough people to populate the future Fascist empire.

For all its efforts, however, in political and economic terms, the regime lost the Battle for Births. Before 1937, the marriage rate did not increase and the birth rate steadily declined. Most Italians were not persuaded to have more children. A shortage of non-manual jobs in some areas and the low living standards of many urban and rural workers encouraged later marriages and discouraged bigger families. The desire for a comfortable lifestyle, particularly in the towns and cities, also explains why the government's message went largely unheeded.

Glossary

Autarky

National economic self-sufficiency.

Ersatz goods

Artificial and often inferior substitutes for imported materials – such as rayon for cotton and lanital (made from milk) for wool. This could not compensate for Italy's serious shortage of raw materials, particularly coal, iron and oil. By 1939 domestic production accounted for only 20% of the nation's raw material needs.

Cartel

A cartel is a group of companies in the same industry or related industries which join together in a single organisation. The chemical giant Montecatini, for example, was an industrial empire, comprising 43 firms, 188 plants and 64,000 workers.

The Battle for Births		
Mussolini's ideal Italian family	2 parents and 12 children	
Population of Italy	40m (1927)	44.5m (1940)
Number of live births per 1000 women of child-bearing age	147.5 (1911)	102.7 (1936)
'Bachelor' tax	1m unmarried men (1939) – 230m lire raised (1939)	

The population increased at a modest rate to 44.5 million in 1940 and 47.5 million in 1950, well short of the *Duce*'s target. As a result, Mussolini's claim that the Italian army could rely on 'eight million bayonets' remained empty propaganda.

Fascism and agriculture

In agriculture as well, Mussolini pursued measures to strengthen his political position, demonstrate Italy's great power status and make the nation self-sufficient for war. In 1925, the regime launched the Battle for Grain to remove Italy's traditional reliance on grain imports. The *Duce* feared that, in war, foreign supplies could be cut off and the nation starved into submission. Buying in foreign wheat also contributed to Italy's balance of trade deficit. To solve these problems, a patriotic campaign to maximise domestic grain production was started. The state offered equipment grants and agricultural advice to farmers who cultivated wheat, guaranteed a generous price for their produce and imposed a high tariff on foreign grain.

The Battle for Grain curtailed wheat imports by 75% between 1925 and 1935. It also improved average harvests from 5.39 million tons in the early 1920s to 7.27 million tons a decade later. Cereal production doubled from 1922 to 1939 and, by the late 1930s, Italy cultivated enough grain to feed itself. Mussolini extracted much propaganda value and important political support from this successful initiative but there was a downside. Wheat grown in parts of southern and central Italy – where the soil and climate did not favour grain – displaced the traditional rural export industries of citrus, wine and olive oil production. Furthermore, high tariffs and guaranteed prices protected inefficient farmers, slowed down agricultural mechanisation and made bread more expensive.

In 1928 the 'Mussolini Law' committed the dictatorship to generously funded, comprehensive land reclamation and led to successful projects in Tuscany and the area around Rome. The Pontine Marshes were the propaganda showpiece of this policy. By 1935 they had been drained and converted into small farms run by ex-servicemen. This project, just 56 kilometres from Rome, provided the regime with much favourable publicity as it could be easily reached by foreign journalists and visiting agricultural experts. Land reclamation also improved public health (by reducing malaria and providing clean drinking water) and created one-third of all public works jobs during the Depression. Overall though, the economic impact of this initiative was limited. Barely 5% of the designated 4.75 million hectares was 'reclaimed' and the scheme settled fewer than 10,000 landless peasants.

In 1927 Mussolini also announced his intention to '**ruralise**' Italy by establishing a new pro-Fascist class of productive small peasant landowners, but this proved to be an economic and political failure. New and potential peasant landowners were adversely affected by deflation after 1926 (which brought falling food prices and mortgage payment problems) and a shortage of rural credit facilities. As a result, the number of peasant landowners shrank from around 3.4 million to under 3 million between 1921 and 1936. During the Fascist era as a whole, over 500,000 peasant farmers left agriculture.

Incentives in the Battle for Births

- Generous allowances and tax exemptions for larger families (no income tax if the family had ten children).
- Marriage loans that were part paid-off with each child (fully paid off with four children).
- Civil service jobs reserved for married fathers.

Sanctions

- Heavy taxation on bachelors.
- Pressure on women to stay at home.
- The 1931 penal code criminalised those who conducted abortions or promoted contraception.

Glossary

Gross national product (GNP)

The monetary value of all that is produced (goods and services) in a country in one year.

The Fascist economy up to 1939: winners and losers

Fascist economic policy had some success. Italy was generally more prosperous in 1939 than in 1923 due to an average annual rise in **gross national product** of 1.2%. By 1939, industrial production had increased by over 145% since 1913 and was 20% above the level achieved in the immediate pre-Depression years. This was reinforced by a modest improvement in average wages (1913 index 100 rose to 121 in 1928 and 125 in 1934). Fascist measures did not always have a positive impact though. Military and welfare spending consumed 15 billion and 6.7 billion lire per year respectively at the end of the decade, putting the state under massive financial strain. Moreover, government agencies – which by the late 1930s controlled key sectors of the economy, including electricity, armaments, shipbuilding and steel – encouraged political intervention, stifled entrepreneurial initiative and made important industries completely reliant on the state. Italy also continued to lag behind her major European competitors in terms of industrial output and economic growth. Wheat production had doubled by the Second World War, but at the expense of traditional agricultural export industries and livestock numbers. Mussolini's policies also failed to tackle rural poverty and the backwardness of southern agriculture.

Economic growth rate per head, 1922–38	
Country	% per year
Italy	1.9
Germany	3.8
Britain	2.2
Western Europe average	2.5

The agricultural population in Italy 1901–1936				
	Peasant landholders	Tenant farmers	Sharecroppers	Peasant workers
1901	2.6 million	0.8 million	2 million	4.2 million
1921	3.4 million	0.7 million	1.6 million	4.5 million
1936	2.9 million	1.6 million	1.8 million	2.4 million

The industrialists and large landowners gained most from the regime's economic measures, which protected their products and profits, and controlled urban and rural manual workers. Large sections of the urban middle class also benefited. By increasing the number of civil servants, teachers and public employees from 500,000 to one million, Mussolini offered the better educated the prospect of secure state service jobs. Moreover, measures to restrain organised labour gave the urban middle class a sense of protection and status.

Their rural counterparts – peasant landholders, tenant farmers and sharecroppers – fared less well. Peasant landholding declined during the Fascist period and, although the number of tenant farmers and sharecroppers increased, the landowners imposed stricter terms and conditions on them. Rural and urban workers were adversely affected too. In the early 1930s the wages of agricultural labourers were cut by between 20 and 40%, which prompted many peasant workers to defy government restrictions on their movement and leave their villages for the city slums.

Fascism and ruralism

Mussolini's attempts to 'ruralise' Italy were linked to self-sufficiency and land reclamation but also reflected wider aims. Rural Italians had more children. The regime hoped this would compensate for the declining birth rate in industrial and urban areas and produce the peasant soldiers required to win and colonise the empire. In addition, Fascist ideology regarded rural life as healthier and morally superior to urban living: in 1928, Mussolini launched an official 'empty the cities' campaign (backed by the prefects and police) to prevent migration to urban areas.

Nevertheless, the regime's attempts to stem urban growth, boost the population and expand the peasant farming sector made little headway against the long-term trends of a falling birth rate and the shift to an urban-industrial society. Ironically, some Fascist policies also undermined the *Duce's* mission to 'ruralise' the nation. The 'Battle for Grain', for instance, hardly encouraged the repopulation of the countryside when wheat was best cultivated on the large-scale mechanised commercial farms of the Po Valley, which required fewer workers.

Allied bombing of Italy

By September 1943, some 21,000 Italians had been killed in British and American bombing raids. These mass aerial attacks, particularly in northern Italy, demoralised the population, disrupted war production and drove thousands out of the cities. During 1942, 25,000 dwellings were destroyed in Turin and 500,000 people fled from Milan. Other strategic centres, including Rome, Genoa and Naples, were also targeted. Naples, for example, was bombed 180 times by the US air force in 1943. These raids generated much popular anger against the Fascist government and its alliance with the Third Reich.

Between 1922 and 1939, industrial wages fell by 14% and, in 1936, even Mussolini admitted that Italians faced the prospect of lower living standards. In addition, the Corporate State usually favoured the employers over the workers. To some extent, however, the hardship experienced by the working class was offset by periodic price cuts and the availability of social security benefits. The syndicates also offered industrial workers some economic protection by successfully pursuing wage claims and other improvements such as welfare payments. Most working-class Italians still resented Fascism for destroying the trade unions and defeating socialism but broadly accepted that Mussolini's policies had sheltered them from the worst of the Depression.

The war economy 1940–43

Italy's disastrous performance in the Second World War highlighted its economic weakness. Inadequate supplies of fuel and raw materials restricted production and forced the regime to rely heavily on limited quantities of coal from Nazi Germany. Annual steel production fell from 2.3 million tons (1938) to 1.7 million tons (1943), and the number of vehicles manufactured halved between 1938 and 1941. Many factories could not obtain essential resources.

These problems were compounded by the systematic bombing of Italy's major industrial centres from late 1942, which disrupted production, demoralised the workers and forced thousands to abandon the cities. Wartime shortages of heating fuel and consumer goods also damaged morale. Furthermore, although real wages were broadly maintained and family allowances increased, the working week was extended to at least 48 hours and the government rationing system provided an inadequate diet of just 1000 calories per day.

Under such circumstances, the black market thrived. The food shortages were partly due to the large number of peasants serving in the army and the drying-up of supplies of animal feed and artificial fertilizers after 1941. Many farmers made the situation worse by eating their own produce or trading it on the black market instead of selling it at fixed prices to the official agencies.

Livorno in ruins after the German retreat, September 1944

The Fascist regime and other groups

The industrialists

Fascism had come to power with the backing of the **industrial** and **agricultural** elites and their continued support was required to realise Mussolini's vision of a militarised, self-sufficient imperial Italy. For their part, industrialists and landowners looked to the regime to protect their political and economic interests by marginalising socialism, controlling the workers, maintaining private ownership and safeguarding their markets. After 1926, Fascist measures designed to protect and boost the heavy industry sector consolidated the industrialists' support. The Corporate State also favoured business interests because, from 1928, workers in the corporations were represented by PNF officials who were usually pro-employer. Furthermore, the industrialists could negotiate directly with the regime through autonomous bodies such as *Confindustria* and were regularly consulted on economic issues.

Beneath the common outlook, though, there were disagreements. The business community wanted to revalue the lira but some industrialists felt that 'Quota 90' was set too high and would damage Italy's economic prospects. Moreover, by the late 1930s some business leaders were so concerned about the state of the economy and the pro-Nazi direction of the regime that they began transferring their money to Swiss bank accounts. Most industrialists, however, continued until the early 1940s to support a Fascist system which guaranteed contracts and high returns. During the early stages of the Second World War, industrialists continued to make large profits and hoped to take commercial advantage of Italy's expected territorial gains.

Unfortunately for Mussolini, later wartime events eroded the industrial elite's support for the Fascist system. The regime could not prevent the Allied bombing in 1942–43 which destroyed the industrialists' factories and badly disrupted production. The strikes of March 1943, involving over 100,000 workers in Piedmont and Lombardy, also alarmed business leaders. These stoppages, with their economic and anti-Fascist political demands, further discredited the regime in the eyes of the industrialists because it no longer appeared able to control the workforce. Industrialists probably played no direct role in Mussolini's removal from power in July 1943 (see below) but by then they clearly regarded the regime as a liability and the king's appointment of a non-Fascist military government reassured them that their businesses would remain under private management.

The landowners

The Fascist dictatorship relied just as much on the *agrari* of the Po Valley and the large landowners from other regions. Mussolini needed their grain to help create a self-sufficient Italy capable of waging a successful war. Their established political influence in the provinces was also required to consolidate Fascist rule as the Battle for the South amply demonstrated (see below). The *agrari* were the real victors in the Battle for Grain, which bolstered their profits and entrenched their local economic power.

Fascist measures that benefited industrialists

- The Battle for Grain, which promoted intensive farming in northern Italy, offered new commercial opportunities to industrial cartels such as FIAT (who made tractors) and Montecatini (who supplied fertilisers).

- In 1929 Mussolini backed *Confindustria* and rejected the syndicates' call for Fascist agents to monitor working conditions in the factories. *Confindustria* argued that such a move would undermine the employers' authority and lower production.

- A law of June 1932 enabled existing producers in a particular economic sector to form cartels which limited competition and maintained prices.

- A licensing law, introduced in January 1933, worked in a similar way by curbing competition and protecting the markets of established firms.

Glossary

Podestas

Appointed officials who replaced elected mayors in 1926. They were chosen by the prefects.

Fascist measures that benefited landowners

- In 1924, FISA (the fascist farmers' union) merged with CONFAG (the existing agricultural organisation). This guaranteed the commercial *agrari* of the Po Valley and the southern landowners an influential voice.
- As part of the Battle for Grain, wheat tariffs were introduced in 1925, 1928 and 1929 to protect home producers.
- Mussolini preserved the *agrari*'s estates: in 1930 the large landowners accounted for just 0.5% of the population but owned almost 42% of the land.
- The Charter of the *Mezzadria* in 1933 increased the landowners' powers over sharecroppers regarding tenancies and contracts.
- The government passed measures to guarantee the *agrari* a large pool of cheap rural labour: in 1930 peasants had to obtain the local prefect's permission to move to a city and in 1935 special workbooks were introduced to control rural migration.

The progressive landowners of the Po Valley were able to increase their crop yields and prices within a protected home market. Tariffs on imported wheat helped the less efficient *agrari* of the south too and allowed them to survive without modernising their estates. In addition, the government put groups of *agrari* in charge of their own state-subsidised land reclamation schemes. Over ten years these landowners received around 4 billion lire to fund such projects. The old agrarian notables retained their local political importance as well. Most of the 7000 **podestas** appointed to run the municipalities were landowners and in Tuscany they were often drawn from the local nobility. In southern Italy, where many Fascist branches were established in 1926, the *agrari* became local party leaders. This gave some substance to the anti-Fascist taunt that the PNF was simply 'the old ruling class in black shirts'.

Merger with the Nationalists, 1923

Perhaps Mussolini's most surprising early act as prime minister was to amalgamate the PNF with Luigi Federzoni's small but influential Nationalist Association (ANI). During the March on Rome, the Nationalists' **Blueshirt** squads had stood ready to fight the Fascists on the king's command. Mussolini always regarded the February 1923 agreement as a 'marriage of convenience', but it offered several advantages. The pro-Catholic ANI pursued a patriotic, monarchist, anti-liberal agenda and contained a larger pool of political and administrative talent than the PNF. It was also stronger in the South, had valuable business, military and royal connections and gave the Fascists greater respectability. By absorbing the 80,000-strong *Sempre Pronti* into the Fascist Militia, the Blueshirt threat was neutralised as well.

The Nationalists were to have a significant impact on the regime's development. The merger enabled the PNF to extend its political influence down the Italian peninsula and win the Battle for the South. Furthermore, Federzoni and another leading Nationalist, Alfredo Rocco, played key roles in shaping the structure of the Fascist state. As minister of the interior (1924–26), Federzoni introduced a series of repressive measures to strengthen the regime including press censorship, the abolition of elected mayors and greater public security. Rocco, the minister of justice from 1925 to 1932, became, in Mussolini's words, 'the legislator of the fascist revolution'. He introduced the death penalty, imposed restrictions on the press and opposition parties, and brought the workers firmly under state control with the Rocco Law (1926) and the Labour Charter (1927). Rocco was also responsible for the penal code of 1931, much of which survived the Second World War.

The civil service and judiciary

Mussolini refused to replace the existing personnel in key state institutions with PNF appointees, as the Fascist radicals demanded. There was to be no 'Fascist revolution' in government. Such a policy would have weakened his own position by bringing about a damaging conflict with these institutions and strengthening the party's influence. Mussolini also recognised that the conservatively inclined senior civil servants, judges and generals mostly endorsed his regime. To bolster this support, he introduced policies which these elite groups could accept, made promotion dependent on loyalty and threatened to deal ruthlessly with any opposition from the state institutions.

Conservative career officials continued to dominate the bureaucracy, prompting the PNF to complain in 1927 that only 15% of civil servants were Fascists. Even in the new Fascist Ministry of Corporations in 1938 all the senior officials had been civil servants since 1916. Nonetheless, the bureaucrats dutifully implemented Mussolini's policies. By the early 1930s, many civil servants had joined the PNF, mainly because promotion depended on it, and from 1935 party membership became a condition of employment. The regime also increased the number of civil service jobs to attract middle-class Italians.

Although Mussolini claimed that he never interfered with the judiciary, this institution was purged. Numerous judges, barristers and solicitors were removed because of 'political incompatibility'. The judiciary was expected to do the government's bidding and, therefore, the Italian legal system lost all claim to impartiality. Mussolini intervened in several court cases, most notably that of the Communist Antonio Gramsci (see page 71), and many suspects were imprisoned without a trial.

The army

Action was also taken to secure the army leadership's loyalty. This, of course, was vital both for the regime's domestic survival and the successful pursuit of an expansionist foreign policy. In return for their support, the generals wanted the freedom to run military affairs without interference from the PNF and the militia. In short, most senior army and navy officers wanted to return to the life they had enjoyed before 1915. It was a price the *Duce* was willing to pay to achieve his territorial ambitions.

Mussolini's retention of the monarchy smoothed relations because the military remained loyal to the king and regarded the crown as an important symbol of national unity, tradition and state authority. Senior officers were also pleased when the MVSN, which they feared might become an alternative Fascist 'people's army', was placed under greater army control in August 1924. For good measure, in September 1925, General Gonzaga was appointed commander of the militia. In the same year, Mussolini calmed service and royal nerves by overruling proposed military cuts and sacking the war minister who advocated them. Other measures in the mid-1920s provided further reassurance. The old 'garrison' army structure was restored, officers' pay was boosted, the coveted senior rank of marshall was created (1924), and Mussolini became his own war, air and navy minister (1925–29 and 1933–43). From then on, in practice, the three armed services were run by under-secretaries who were usually generals or admirals. The appointment of **Pietro Badoglio**, a monarchist career soldier comfortable with the regime, as chief of the general staff in 1925 also made for good relations between the government and the military.

Glossary

Blueshirts

The ANI's paramilitary force, the *Sempre Pronti* (Ever Ready), whose uniform was a blue shirt.

Biography

Pietro Badoglio
(1871–1956)

After joining the Italian army in 1890, Badoglio served in Abyssinia (1896) and the Italo-Turkish war (1911–12). During the First World War, he was responsible for the successful capture of Monte Sabotino (1916) and, although his forces were defeated at Caporetto (1917), Badoglio emerged from the conflict as a prominent general. He was chief of the general staff 1919–21 and again from 1925. A year later he was made a field marshall. After serving as governor of Libya (1928–34), Badoglio commanded the Italian forces in Abyssinia (1935–36) and captured the capital, Addis Ababa. He disagreed with Mussolini in 1940 over Italy's preparations for entering the Second World War. In December 1940, during Italy's disastrous campaign in Greece, Badoglio resigned and dissociated himself from the *Duce*'s actions. He played an important role in the overthrow of Mussolini in July 1943 and then, as prime minister, announced Italy's unconditional surrender to the Allies.

Consequently, there was no systematic Fascist takeover of the army's upper ranks. Indeed, as late as December 1940, the regime was still trying to get army officers to join the PNF. Having said this, the regime and the generals both wanted army expansion and a more assertive foreign policy. In essence, the Fascist state maintained the jobs of career soldiers and ensured their support but at the expense of proper military planning, co-ordination and efficiency. Badoglio, for example, made no serious attempt to co-ordinate the three services, underestimated the value of tanks and did not press ahead with technological improvements. Each branch competed for resources and rejected the inter-service collaboration and combined operations required for a major war. Military academies were outdated and there were far too many senior officers. In 1939 the army had 600 generals. These and other shortcomings would become painfully clear during the Second World War.

Local government

At local level, Mussolini reinforced the prefects' authority at the expense of regional Fascist leaders. Of the 86 prefects appointed in the years between 1922 and 1929, 57 were career bureaucrats and just 29 were Fascists. The latter were usually sent to less-important areas. In 1926, elected local councils were abolished and each prefect now nominated the *podestas* in his province. Generally, they opted for prosperous landowners and ex-military officers rather than local Fascists, partly because most *podestas* were not paid. Mussolini also issued directives insisting that the prefect, not the regional party secretary, controlled the province. By mid-1927, this appeared to apply in about 81 of the 91 provinces, but disputes between prefects and local party bosses continued.

The Battle for the South

Traditionally, southern Italy was dominated by well-connected local political elites (including large landowners) who controlled the municipal councils and offered patronage in return for votes. Initially, PNF attempts to establish southern *fasci* had had little impact because they lacked local allies and influence. When the ANI was absorbed into the PNF, however, Fascism's prospects in the South were transformed. Pro-Nationalist notables and their local followings moved over to the Fascist Party. This strengthened the PNF's position but at the cost of compromising with the local political elites, accepting their continued dominance in local affairs and abandoning Fascist radicalism.

Once in government, the PNF was also able to win over southern liberals and their local supporters by offering access to patronage and the resources of the state. For this reason, during the coalition period, Mussolini appointed prominent southern politicians to run ministries (such as the Ministry of Public Works) which funded thousands of jobs in the South. On a local level, prefects used their provincial powers over public spending, public sector employment and municipal councils to persuade members of the local elite to join the PNF. Only a few liberal leaders resisted.

After the Acerbo Law of 1923 (see page 163), candidates for parliament stood a much better chance of being elected if they were on the government's officially endorsed list. Consequently, many southern politicians and deputies joined it, bringing their local support with them. Non-Fascists on the list lost their political independence in the PNF bloc. These right-wing, liberal and Catholic 'flankers' formed a significant proportion of the government's candidates in the South.

Mussolini and the king

Mussolini remained outwardly deferential towards the king, visiting him twice a week and accepting royal advice on appointments and honours. Victor Emmanuel was even made Emperor of Abyssinia in 1936. After all, as head of state, he could still sack Mussolini, suppress the PNF and turn elite opinion against Fascism. Fortunately for Mussolini, though, the king was a weak and insecure man with little faith in liberal politicians. He felt he needed the Fascist leader's support to retain the throne. Accordingly, the king signed Mussolini's decrees and did not openly oppose measures he disliked. Underneath the public image of friendship, however, there was much resentment. Victor Emmanuel regarded Mussolini as a 'vulgar and offensive' usurper of royal powers and, privately, the *Duce* derided 'this tiresome monarchy'. By 1930, the king had virtually withdrawn from public affairs and royal influence was weak.

Mussolini weakened the king's influence in a number of ways:

- In December 1928, the Grand Council acquired the right to be consulted over the royal succession and to compile the list from which the monarch would choose the next thehead of government.

- In April 1938, the newly created title First Marshall of the Empire was given to both Victor Emmanuel and Mussolini, which appeared to give the head of state and the head of government equal status.

- In January 1939, the law replacing the Chamber of Deputies with the Chamber of Fasces and Corporations did not mention the king's role in the law-making process.

- In June 1940, Mussolini weakened the king's position as commander-in-chief by assuming operational command of the Italian army.

Mussolini confided to senior Fascists in the later 1930s that he wanted to abolish the monarchy. He hoped that a successful war, in alliance with Nazi Germany, would boost the popularity of the Fascist system and allow him to remove the Crown's powers. Victor Emmanuel, in contrast, was unenthusiastic about the *Duce*'s pro-Axis foreign policy, which made him an obvious potential rallying point for those unhappy with the regime. The king concluded that Italy's involvement in the Second World War would mean the end of the Italian monarchy. A Fascist victory would enable Mussolini to dismantle the monarchy. Defeat, on the other hand, would leave the Crown compromised in the eyes of the Allies because of its association with the dictatorship.

Mussolini's downfall in 1943, however, indicates that the king continued to have at least a limited constitutional role, one which assumed greater importance as Mussolini's influence waned with military defeats.

The king and Mussolini's downfall

By mid-1943, Italy's disastrous performance in the war had led to an almost complete loss of confidence in Mussolini's leadership. Earlier in the year, the king's advisers began discussions with army generals and police chiefs about royal action but a firm decision to remove Mussolini was probably only taken in mid-July. Furthermore, prominent moderate Fascists, such as Grandi, wanted to end Mussolini's personal dictatorship and the alliance with Germany. They were mainly motivated by Italy's dire military position but Mussolini's decision to remove some of them from their posts in February 1943 sharpened their opposition. At the Fascist Grand Council meeting of 24–25 July 1943, Grandi put forward a resolution calling for the king to assume full command of the Italian forces and for the proper functioning of government institutions. The motion, which was carried by 19 votes to 7, amounted to a vote of no confidence in Mussolini's personal leadership but seemed to imply that a collective Fascist government could carry on. Later on 25th July, Victor Emmanuel dismissed the *Duce*. The king informed Mussolini that the army's morale had completely collapsed and that the dictator was now 'the most hated man in Italy'.

Chamber of Deputies

From 1926, Italy was a one-party state and only PNF deputies sat in the Chamber. Parliament was further weakened in May 1928 when a new law changed the composition of the lower house: the Chamber would now consist of 400 deputies chosen by the Grand Council from 1000 candidates put forward by the national syndical confederations and other approved bodies. Thus the whole selection process rested with the PNF and the government. The public were then to approve or reject the deputies *en bloc* in a plebiscite. In March 1929, in the first plebiscite held under the new system, over 8.5 million Italians approved the deputy list and just 137,761 registered their opposition. Eventually, in January 1939, another law replaced the lower house with the Chamber of Fasces and Corporations, which was made up of members of the Grand Council, the National Council of Corporations and the PNF National Council. This strengthened the government's hand by turning the Chamber into an assembly of regime-endorsed officials.

The Senate

In contrast, the Senate, appointed by the king for life and drawn from the traditional elites, remained untouched and continued to function as a forum for debate. Even anti-Fascist senators such as the intellectual Benedetto Croce were tolerated. In 1932, for example, the upper house contained 148 senators who were not associated with the PNF. Mussolini left the Senate alone for two reasons. First, any interference would have been seen as a direct assault on both the monarch's authority and that of the most powerful groups in society. Second, the upper house was a largely compliant body. It had supported Mussolini at crucial points such as June 1924 and had not participated in the parliamentary walk-out during the Matteotti crisis.

The role of the PNF within the Fascist system after 1925

From 1925 to 1926, Mussolini exerted greater **control over the PNF**. The *Duce* was determined to base his dictatorship on Italy's existing state institutions rather than the Fascist Party for a number of reasons:

- he wanted to rule without party interference in decision-making

- he feared that the radicalism of the PNF intransigents would alienate important backers, including the industrialists and large landowners

- the PNF lacked the experienced administrators required to run the machinery of state.

Consequently, several measures were introduced from the mid-1920s to subordinate the party to Mussolini's authority. This enabled the *Duce* to appoint compliant senior PNF officials such as Achille Starace, who was national party secretary 1931–39. Party membership increased over this period as many civil servants joined the PNF for job-related rather than ideological reasons. As a result, the party became a bloated bureaucracy mainly staffed by careerists who lacked both Fascist convictions and dynamism. Although deprived of a policy-making role, the PNF was given another function: to

---

Key measures to control the PNF

- 1925–26 PNF centralised to reduce the power of the provincial Fascist leaders.
- PNF Congress did not meet after 1925.
- 1926 Party Statute formally made Mussolini head of the PNF and stated that all party appointments had to be made by PNF headquarters in Rome, not chosen locally.
- 1926–31 some 170,000 mainly intransigent members were expelled from the PNF.

PNF membership	
Year	**Members**
1922	477,000
1923	783,000
1927	1,262,834
1930	1,723,400
1934	1,851,000
1939	2,633,000

turn Italians into enthusiastic Fascists. To achieve this, the party became an important channel for the regime's propaganda. By developing and extending a national network of mass organisations (which included the ONB and the OND – see page 67–68), the party aimed to instil patriotic and military values into the Italian character and foster public identification with Fascism through a range of sporting, leisure and welfare activities.

Fascist Italy and the Catholic Church

The Lateran Pacts, 1929

Mussolini knew he needed Catholic support to govern Italy. As the head of the Church, the pope commanded enormous authority and respect, both domestically and internationally. Furthermore, around 90% of Italians regarded themselves as Catholic and about 30% were regular churchgoers.

Once in power, Mussolini continued to woo the Catholic Church by placing crucifixes in state buildings, introducing religious education into state primary schools, baling out the Catholic Bank of Rome, and discouraging Freemasonry. In January 1923, he began secret talks with Cardinal Pietro Gasparri, the Vatican secretary of state. He remained anti-clerical and an atheist but realised that an agreement with the papacy would increase his personal popularity and raise the regime's international and domestic standing. For its part, the Vatican concluded that a stable authoritarian state would allow Catholicism to thrive by curbing socialism and liberalism, promoting order, and respecting traditional values. Mussolini had to proceed cautiously though. Many prominent Fascists were anti-religious and regarded the Church's youth organisation, Catholic Action (see page 21), as an anti-Fascist body. The king also had little time for the Church and would oppose any move to strengthen the pope's political influence or hand territory to the Vatican.

Negotiations for a wide-ranging settlement commenced in 1926 and, after three years of tough bargaining, **the Lateran Pacts** were signed in February 1929. This agreement, containing a treaty, a financial convention and a **concordat**, resolved the political dispute between the Italian government and the papacy which had dogged Church–state relations since 1870.

The Lateran Pacts were Mussolini's greatest domestic achievement. Pope Pius XI praised him as the 'man whom providence has sent us' and Catholics everywhere hailed the *Duce* for the 'great reconciliation'. For Mussolini, though, it was just another necessary compromise to secure his dictatorship. In his view, the agreement turned Catholicism into an important ally and excluded the Church from Italian politics. It also revealed the limits of Mussolini's power: he had to accept the pope's unique position and accommodate the most powerful conservative force in Italian society.

The Lateran Pacts

The pope formally recognised the Italian state, including the old Papal States and Rome. The state, in return, acknowledged the pope's sovereignty over the Vatican City and paid 750 million lire (about £35 million) – plus 1000 million lire in bonds – in compensation to the papacy for renouncing its claim to Rome and the loss of former papal lands. Under the concordat, Catholicism became Italy's state religion and acquired privileged status. Religious education became compulsory in state secondary schools, Catholic Action continued to function, and the pope was to nominate all bishops. The clergy would receive state-funded salaries but could not join political parties. Moreover, civil marriage was no longer a legal requirement and no-one could divorce without the Church's consent.

Glossary

Concordat

A formal agreement between the Catholic Church and a nation state, which recognises a special role of the Church in the life of a nation. It also implies papal approval of the government of that nation.

> **Take note**
>
> Assess the impact of the Lateran Pacts of 1929 on the regime.

Church-State relations after 1929

After 1929, the Church generally provided valuable support for the regime, which was epitomised by the official slogan 'For Pope and *Duce'*. The Catholic hierarchy applauded Mussolini's military ventures in Abyssinia and Spain in the 1930s as campaigns against heathenism and communism. Priests became involved in Fascist initiatives such as the ONB and campaigns against the 'decadence' of modern dancing, fashion and films. Clergy also praised the *Duce* in their pastoral letters and often gave the Fascist salute. Underneath the surface, however, Church–state tensions remained. Many radical Fascists regarded the agreement with the papacy as a major obstacle to the creation of a Fascist totalitarian state. Some of the clergy also had reservations about the Church's close relationship with Mussolini's regime. When, for example, the Archbishop of Milan publicly endorsed the *Duce's* government in 1930, some 300 priests reacted by signing an open letter which stressed that Catholicism and Fascism were incompatible.

In 1931 the government closed down Catholic Action (which by then possessed some 700,000 members) because the authorities suspected that the organisation was simply a sanctuary for Catholic anti-Fascism. In response, the pope issued an **encyclical** which accused the PNF of 'pagan worship of the state'. Eventually, in September 1931, an uneasy compromise was agreed which reopened Catholic Action for religious and non-sporting activities only. A second major disagreement took place in 1937–38 over the regime's growing anti-Semitism. The pope openly condemned racial discrimination and the Vatican argued that the anti-Semitic laws broke the terms of the 1929 Lateran Pacts since they prohibited mixed marriages between Catholics and Jews, including converted Jews.

Overall, the 1929 agreement with the Catholic Church greatly boosted the *Duce's* popularity and helped the dictatorship to achieve broad political acceptance in the early 1930s. Nevertheless, the Church secured longer-term advantages that undermined the regime's attempts to forge a totalitarian state. This was due to a resurgence in Catholicism during these years. The number of clergy and Church schools increased and Catholic Action's membership reached one million. Furthermore, the Catholic students' federation, FUCI, provided a rival social and cultural forum for undergraduates. The growth of Catholic influence through a variety of institutions in the 1930s offered many Italians an alternative to the Fascist vision of society (particularly over issues such as militarism and respect for human life) and hindered Mussolini's drive to establish a regimented Fascist nation. By 1943, as Italy's war went from bad to worse, the Vatican cautiously began to reposition itself. The Catholic Church secretly used its contacts with the US government to make the king aware that a separate peace with the Allies could be discussed if he appointed an anti-Nazi and non-communist government.

Glossary

Encyclical

A letter from the pope sent to all Catholic bishops.

Resurgence of Catholicism		
Pupils in Church-run secondary schools	31,000 (1927)	104,000 (1940)
Number of clergy	68,264 (1921)	70,652 (1931)
Number of nuns	71,000 (1921)	129,000 (1936)

Conclusion: Was the Fascist state a success?

The Fascist regime did deliver modest economic growth and protected the interests of industrialists, large landowners and, to a lesser extent, the urban middle class. Overall though, Fascist economic policy was a failure. The Corporate State was supposed to herald a new 'third way' between capitalism and communism but its impact on the Italian economy was minimal. In addition, rural and urban workers' living standards suffered. Crucially, Mussolini's drive for autarky to prepare Italy for war also made little progress beyond the Battle for Grain and the state support given to heavy industry. Throughout the 1920s and 1930s, economic self-sufficiency remained an unattainable ideal.

Mussolini's policies, however, were successful in gaining the support or compliance of the elites for much of this period. The *Duce* came to terms with the dominant groups in Italian society because he knew he could not exercise political power if they opposed him. Moreover, Mussolini recognised that the elites were central to the achievement of the Fascist dictatorship's domestic and foreign aims. For their part, the key groups were prepared to be absorbed into the Fascist system since it gave them privileged status and protected their interests. This alliance between Mussolini and the elites lasted until the Second World War. By 1942–43, Italy's disastrous military performance put the elites' loyalty under growing strain and they began to distance themselves from the regime.

Activity: Was the Fascist state a success?

One way to assess the Fascist state's success or failure is to compare its achievements with its aims. Use your knowledge and understanding of Mussolini's domestic policies to complete, in detail, a table considering the following aims:

- a self-sufficient economy
- 'ruralise' Italy
- win over Italy's elite groups
- secure the support of the Catholic Church.

How far does this evidence suggest that the Fascist state was a success?

Taking it further

To find out more about the Fascist economy, see Chapter 7 of *Fascist Italy* by John Hite and Chris Hinton (John Murray, 1998) and pages 60–65 of *Fascist Italy* by John Whittam (Manchester University Press, 1995).

To find out more about the Italian elites and their relationship with the Fascist regime, see Alexander De Grand, *Italian Fascism: Its Origins & Development* (University of Nebraska, 1982), pages 46–49 and 124–25.

A short, informative account of the Lateran Pacts can be found in Philip Morgan, *Italian Fascism 1919–1945* (Macmillan, 1995), pages 95–97.

Skills Builder 3: **Writing introductions and conclusions**

When answering questions in Unit 1, students will be expected to write an essay. In this third Skills Builder, we will be looking at the importance of writing introductory and concluding paragraphs.

When writing under examination conditions, you should spend approximately 40 minutes on the whole of your essay. During this time you must:

- plan what you are going to write
- write a separate paragraph for each major point you wish to make
- check through what you have written.

Therefore, given the time constraints, you should not spend more than five minutes writing your introduction.

What should you put in your introduction?

Your introduction should answer the question directly and set out what you plan to cover and discuss in your essay. Your introduction needs to show that you will answer the question in an analytical way – and that you haven't just started writing without thinking. Therefore, it is good to say, very briefly, what you are going to argue in the essay. You can then refer back to your introduction as you write, to make sure that your argument is on track.

We are going to look at an introduction to an answer to the following question:

> (A) How far do you agree that the use of repression was the main reason the Fascist regime was able to control Italy in the years 1925–43?

This question gives one of the commonly quoted reasons for Fascist control of Italy, and it asks you 'how far' you agree that it was the most important reason. This will require you to assess other reasons why the Fascist regime was able to control Italy and make judgments about the significance of each reason in bringing it about.

Here is an example of an introduction that you might write:

State repression was clearly an important factor in the Fascist regime's ability to control Italy from the mid-1920s. As Mussolini's dictatorship was established in 1925–26, various instruments of repression, such as the OVRA and the Special Tribunal, were introduced to target political opponents and keep the Italian population in line. However, Fascist rule was not simply based on coercion and intimidation. Fascist propaganda had some success in persuading many Italians to view the regime in a positive light. The cult of the Duce and organisations such as the OND, in particular, encouraged general public acceptance of the Fascist system. Indeed, large numbers were not only persuaded by ducismo but also regarded Fascist policies before 1940 as broadly successful. Furthermore, important groups and institutions, including industrialists and the Catholic Church, were prepared to work with Mussolini's government because it protected their interests and offered rewards for their compliance.

This introduction answers the question directly. It recognises that Fascist control of Italy had a number of causes. It states some of these causes, and it briefly explains the complexity of causation.

Activity: **Spot the mistake**

The following introductions have been written in response to Question (A). Each one illustrates a common mistake. Spot them!

Example 1

There were many factors that enabled the Fascist regime to control Italy between 1925 and 1943. Fascist propaganda measures encouraged many Italians to view the regime favourably and others concluded that Fascist policies were having a beneficial effect. Italy's elite groups and institutions were reconciled to Fascist rule too because it protected their position and interests.

Example 2

In 1926 a new secret police force, the OVRA, was created under Arturo Bocchini, the chief of police. The OVRA compiled files on potential 'subversives', established a network of informants and carried out raids. A Special Tribunal was also introduced to tackle serious political dissent. Political prisoners now faced the prospect of internal exile (confino) in penal colonies.

Example 3

Fascist rule from the mid-1920s was maintained chiefly by repression. The Fascist regime regarded violence and intimidation as legitimate methods to preserve their power. To coerce the Italian population, by the 1930s the OVRA carried out some 20,000 raids each week and the Special Tribunal imprisoned hundreds of 'political opponents' annually. These and similar techniques ensured that most Italians felt compelled to accept Blackshirt control.

Answers

Example 1 – this introduction considers other factors, but ignores the one in the question.

Example 2 – this introduction describes some of the Fascist regime's repressive measures without answering the question.

Example 3 – this introduction only one possible factor (Fascist repression) and therefore is highly unbalanced and does not show a range of knowledge.

Introductions: DOs and DON'Ts

- DO look at the question and decide on your line of argument.
- DO make reference to the question in your introduction.
- DO show what you intend to argue.
- DON'T begin your answer by writing a story.
- DON'T spend too long writing your introduction. Five minutes is enough.

Why are conclusions important?

When you are asked a question in an examination, you are expected to answer it! The concluding paragraph is very important in this process. It should contain the summary of the argument you have made, with your *verdict* on the question.

Like an introduction, the conclusion should not be more than three or four sentences in length, and under examination conditions it should take no more than five minutes to write. Here is an example of a conclusion for Question (A):

Repression was a constant feature of the regime even though anti-Fascist activity was limited: parliament and the press were controlled, telephone calls and the post were monitored, and Italian society was riddled with police informers. Having said this, the evidence suggests that propaganda initiatives and broadly popular government policies played a more important role than state repression in keeping the Fascists in power. Fascist organisations such as the OND and the cult of the Duce helped the regime achieve a high level of support for much of the 1920s and 1930s. The government's policy successes, such as the Concordat and the conquest of Abyssinia, proved to be very popular with the Italian population and also secured mass backing for Fascist rule; indeed, it was only when military failure dented his popularity that Mussolini's regime lost control.

Activity: Write your own conclusion

(B) How far do you agree that the Catholic Church undermined the Fascist regime in the years 1929–43?

Write a conclusion of not more than four sentences to this question. Try to write it in no more than five minutes.

Chapter 9 **Mussolini's early moves: 1922–33**

Key questions

- What were Mussolini's objectives?
- How did the international situation in 1922–33 affect Mussolini's plans?
- What were Italian weaknesses in competing with foreign powers?
- Was Mussolini's foreign policy in 1922–33 a success or failure?

'The word Italy must prevail over the word Liberty' was a slogan coined by the futurists in 1913. Nationalism and the drive to create a militant national spirit lay at the heart of Mussolini's thinking. In one sense it was all fascism was. Like Crispi and D'Annunzio, Mussolini grieved for the lack of a glorious birth for the new Italy and burned with shame. French and Prussian arms had been instrumental in the victories of the *Risorgimento* and Italy still smarted from the Abyssinian defeat of 1896. Libya had been gained in 1912 but was far from pacified: in 1922 only the coastal towns were under Italian control. The great conflict in the Alps between 1915 and 1918 had been marked by the terrible defeat of Caporetto, and British and French divisions had rushed to the peninsula to prevent wholesale Italian collapse. Well might the British ambassador write in November 1917: 'As for the Italians what can you expect from a nation, the majority of which, would be better employed selling ice cream.'

Take note

Use the map overleaf to identify all the places around the Mediterannean mentioned in the following section.
Why was Britain the dominant power in the area?

Timeline

1922	Washington Naval Treaty
1923	Corfu Affair
1924	Italy gained Fiume
1925	Locarno Treaties
1926	Protectorate declared over Albania
1928	Naval Treaty; Kellogg-Briand Pact
1932	Geneva Disarmament Conference; Grandi dismissed as foreign minister
1933	Four Power Pact with Germany, Britain and France

The pursuit of greatness

Mussolini was determined to win a more martial image for Italians. Italy must cease to be a military joke and become a real great power. Blood must be spilled to create a real nation. There was much talk of a 'warrior education'. The language and rhetoric of fascism was all about struggle, and the virtues of war and the warrior. Violence was not a necessary evil, it was a creative force unlocking rebirth. It was to be welcomed and embraced. In an essay he co-authored in 1932 on the 'Doctrine of Fascism', Mussolini wrote of war being 'the true test of nationhood and manhood'. Mussolini was a talented journalist and much in love with words. There is often a tendency to dismiss his grandiose sentences as just words but he did genuinely believe in the transformation of Italy and the pursuit of national greatness through war. It is a common theme throughout his domestic and foreign policy.

Even during the 1920s, when he is often portrayed as being on his best behaviour and co-operating with the bourgeois powers of Britain and France, he yearned for a war and began to prepare for it.

In real terms, Mussolini set himself and Italy certain territorial goals. Italy, in the long-term, must escape the prison that British and French naval power in the Mediterranean imposed upon it. In 1926, he told a group of senior naval officers:

> '*A nation that has no free access to the sea cannot be considered a free nation; a nation that has no free access to the oceans cannot be considered a great power; Italy must become a great power.*'

Italy was hemmed in by British naval bases, in Malta, Cyprus and, at either end of the Mediterranean, at Gibraltar and Alexandria. France held Corsica and Tunisia, which Italy wanted. Italy could not challenge Britain and France on her own as they were too powerful. The ideal solution was to split them and/or find a powerful ally against one or both of them. The only country suitable as an ally was Germany, as Crispi had envisaged back in the 1880s. However, after the First World War, Germany was too weak. But, in the meantime, Italy could begin to consolidate her hold on existing territories in Libya (North Africa) and also in Somaliland (East Africa). If the whole Mediterranean was ultimately to be turned into an Italian lake, a start could be made by gaining complete control of the Adriatic.

- The port of Fiume, disputed with **Yugoslavia**, could be gained. This had already been tried by D'Annunzio with some success (see page 40).

- With luck, Dalmatia could be torn from Yugoslavia by encouraging **Croat separatism**.

- Adriatic islands like Corfu might be gained from Greece.

Plans could also be laid to expand the East African empire into Ethiopia. It was a demanding and risky agenda.

Yugoslavia and Croat separatism

New state created in 1919. Serbia was at the heart of this new land of the 'united south slavs' and the king of Serbia was head of state. There were considerable tensions in this new country as its various peoples sought independence. There were many cultural differences between the different communities in Yugoslavia. For example, the Slovenes and Croats, who had been part of the Austrian Empire for centuries, were Catholic whereas the Serbians were Greek Orthodox. Many Slovenes and Croats wanted to separate from Yugoslavia.

Italy and the Mediterranean, 1922

Take note

In what ways do the two tables support the opinion that Italy was the least of the great powers?

Italy's economy

The Italian economy was tiny compared to that of Britain and France, let alone the USA. Despite growth in the twentieth century, she was still essentially a rural and peasant society. Italy simply lacked the industrial muscle to be a truly great power. Italian designers and engineers were often brilliant but the country lacked the productive capacity to deliver vast quantities of advanced weaponry. When war eventually came in the 1940s, the US Ford Motor Corporation alone out-produced the whole of Italy in armaments production.

Energy consumption is a good indication of how advanced a country's economy is. Britain's and Germany's steel production had been sharply reduced by the economic slump of the 1930s. However, their potential production was far greater.

Country	Population in 1928 (millions)	Iron/steel in 1930 (million tons)	Energy consumption in 1930 (million tons of coal equivalent)
USA	119.1	41.3	762
Britain	45.7	7.4	184
Germany	55.4	11.3	177
Russia	150.4	5.7	65
France	41	9.4	97.5
Italy	40.3	1.7	24

Industrial output and population of the six major powers in 1928–30

The military balance reflected the economic weakness. In the 1920s Italy increased her military spending, at a time when Britain was savagely cutting her own, but the military balance in 1930 was still heavily against Italy.

Type of ship	Italy	Britain	France
Battleships	4	16	6
Battle cruisers	0	4	0
Aircraft carriers	0	6	1
Heavy cruisers	2	20	6
Cruisers	6	40	9
Destroyers	75	146	70
Submarines	65	50	60

Naval balance 1930

The table on the left sets out the different types of ship in the rival powers' naval forces, in descending size and perceived importance, as a point of comparison.

Militarily, only alliance with another great power – which would have to be Germany as Russia was communist – could allow Italy to risk confrontation with Britain and France, but Germany throughout the 1920s and early 1930s was too weak to counter the Western powers. In addition, Mussolini faced political constraint at home. His power base was insecure and both the army and the king were opposed to risky foreign ventures. Mussolini as yet lacked the grasp on Italian public opinion to overrule these two traditional institutions. The king could dismiss him and the Blackshirt militia lacked the military muscle to confront the army. Mussolini would have to bide his time, but this would not stop him using every opportunity thrown his way to pursue 'greatness'.

Consolidation of the Italian Empire

It is often argued that, for all his and his regime's faults, Mussolini was no mass murderer. Certainly within Italy, there was nothing to compare with the homicidal excesses of Stalin or Hitler. In Africa, however, Mussolini did not seem so benign.

- In Somaliland, De Vecchi – one of the leaders of the March on Rome – earned himself the title 'the Butcher of the Somalis' while he was governor of the province.

- In Libya, the cost of 'pacification' was a far higher body count. General Rodolfo Graziani acted without mercy in the late 1920s to bring western Libya under effective control.

It was the turn of eastern Libya, or Cyrenaica, in 1930. The problem was the nomadic Senussi, who resisted Italian rule, and their leader Omar el Mukhtar. Graziani marched 100,000 civilians, men, women and children, up to a 1000 kilometres to camps on the coast. Stragglers were shot and most of their camels, sheep and goats died. By 1933, 40,000 had died from neglect in these holding camps. El Mukhtar, the Lion of the Desert as he was known to his followers, was captured by Italian troops in 1931 and the 73-year-old was promptly hanged for treason against the Italian state.

European policies 1922–33

Although circumstances forced a certain caution on Mussolini in Europe, his actions showed what he was capable of if circumstances became more favourable. The **French invasion of the Ruhr** in January 1923 gave him the opportunity to risk more in the pursuit of his domination of the Adriatic, as France was looking for diplomatic support against Germany and was therefore more amenable to Italian ambition.

The shooting by Greek assassins of an Italian general and his team while engaged in mapping the Albanian-Greek border produced a typically over-the-top response from Mussolini. Italy seized the Greek island of Corfu in the Adriatic, first shelling it, inflicting several civilian casualties. The outcome was a major international crisis. Italy eventually withdrew on payment by the Greeks of 50 million lire in compensation. The *Duce* refused to have it settled by the new League of Nations, to whom the Greek government had appealed, and it was settled by an ambassadors' conference brokered by Britain. Some see this as a humiliation for the League of Nations and a triumph for Mussolini but, in reality, he had been forced to climb down and withdraw from the island.

Any sense of failure was softened by a real achievement in January 1924, when he got the Yugoslavs to agree to hand over Fiume to Italy. In the light of the previous crisis over the city, this was a real triumph and a boost for the regime. Mussolini's prestige was further enhanced the following year, when the final ending of the Ruhr crisis enabled him to grandstand on the international stage at **Locarno**.

French invasion of the Ruhr, 1923

Tensions in Western Europe were dramatically raised when French and Belgian troops occupied the Ruhr, the most important industrial area of Germany. France aimed to force Germany to keep up the reparation payments as stipulated in the Treaty of Versailles. The invasion produced something of a rift between Britain and France, as Britain did not agree with the invasion.

Glossary

Locarno

This international gathering finally ended the Ruhr crisis and seemed to usher in an era of harmony in Western Europe. France and Germany promised to accept their common borders, i.e. Germany was restating what had been accepted at Versailles, the loss of Alsace-Lorraine and the demilitarisation of the Rhineland, and France was promising not to repeat the invasion of the Ruhr.

Austen Chamberlain

1863–1937

The elder half-brother of the future prime minister, Neville Chamberlain. He was British foreign secretary from 1924 to 1929 and struck up a good working relationship with Mussolini.

Glossary

Protectorate

A weaker country placed under partial control and the official protection of a stronger nation.

Slovenes

Slavic people on the south side of the Alps. They had long been a part of the Austrian Empire and shared much common culture with the Catholic Germans of Austria, but were transferred by the victorious powers at the end of the First World War to the new state of Yugoslavia.

Disarmament

This was the great dream of the 1920s in Britain. Various attempts were made to promote disarmament, most notably the Washington Naval Treaty of 1922. After years of preparation, a full-scale disarmament conference met in Geneva in 1932. Grandi appeared sympathetic to its aims, but his boss was not.

He took part in the negotiations between the French and Germans, and had his ego flattered by the attentions of the British foreign secretary, **Austen Chamberlain**. Mussolini effectively stood as joint guarantor with Britain on the Franco-German border. In doing this, Mussolini appeared to be posing as a champion of international co-operation and peace. This same pose was adopted again in 1928, when Italy agreed to sign the **Kellogg–Briand Pact** of that year. Mussolini was only posing as a friend of peace in both cases. His bellicose policies in the Adriatic revealed his real self and long-term ambitions.

Kellogg–Briand Pact

Idealistic and largely meaningless international agreement proposed by the American and French foreign secretaries. The signatories agreed not to use war as an instrument of policy, but it was soon ignored and broken.

If Yugoslavia thought that the accord over Fiume had bought them Italian goodwill they were very mistaken. Mussolini had designs on Dalmatia, which was also part of Yugoslavia, and began causing trouble in the region. In 1925, Italy turned Albania into a virtual **protectorate** by backing Ahmed bey Zogu's seizure of power. This increased Italian influence in this little country bordering Yugoslavia, and Italian persecution of the small **Slovene** minority in north-east Italy also raised tensions. Yugoslavia rightly felt threatened and upped her military preparations. In November 1927, Yugoslavia signed an alliance with France. Mussolini had already ordered the army to plan for a sudden attack on Yugoslavia and even talked in his wilder moments of a lightning attack on France. Italy had signed an alliance with Hungary and Italian military intelligence began to encourage Macedonian separatists and Croat nationalists, who wished to break away from Yugoslavia, to commit terrorist acts. The aim was to encourage the self-destruction of the new slav country, as out of the wreckage Italy could gain Dalmatia. Mussolini toyed with the idea of war but was firmly told by the army that it would be a disaster and Italy would be crushed by France. The money markets became unstable and the lira's value declined as it was heavily sold in Paris and London. To soothe opinion both at home and abroad, Mussolini gave up the job of foreign minister and appointed the pro-British Dino Grandi (see page 51), in September 1929. Grandi held the position to 1932, but was much too favourably inclined to peace for his boss's taste. Mussolini accused him of going to bed with Britain and France and becoming pregnant with **disarmament**.

Mussolini had no interest in disarmament and, in fact, at a time when Britain and most other powers were disarmed or disarming, Italy's military spending as a percentage of national income went up substantially – from 2.6% in 1923–25 to 5.4% in 1931. The navy's tonnage of warships went up from 400,000 in 1926 to 550,000 in 1933. The air force was also substantially increased. Grandi's removal and replacement by Mussolini in 1932, led to a renewed period of tension with France and Yugoslavia and, once again, there was talk of war. The king and the army chiefs were thoroughly opposed.

Mussolini, in typical fashion, produced a diplomatic rabbit from his hat to deflect attention and cool things down. In March 1933, he put forward a proposal for a 'Four Power Pact'. Britain, France, Italy and Germany would consult and act as mediators in any European wrangle.

Conclusion: Mussolini – war-mongerer or moderator?

Some historians have used the 'Four Power Pact' and Mussolini's role at Locarno to claim that his policy in the first ten years of his rule was moderate and peaceful. Italy also joined the League of Nations. A more accurate guide to his inclinations and intentions, however, were the Corfu crisis of 1923, the tension with Yugoslavia and the increase in defence spending. The wolf may have uttered an imitation baa from time to time but it was still essentially a wolf and not a sheep.

> **Taking it further**
>
> Try to find out more about: Dino Grandi, Ahmed bey Zogu and Omar el Mukhtar. In what ways do their stories exemplify Mussolini's true foreign policy aims?

Activity: Planning for war

In groups of three or four, assume the role of a military planning council for Italy in these years.

1. List potential enemies you might have to go to war with. What are the potential gains and losses from such conflicts?

2. Order the countries in difficulty of defeating in a war, i.e. which is the most dangerous to Italy and which the least?

3. What are the defence implications? What should Italy spend money on: for example, fortifications against France or Yugoslavia, military equipment for the army, ships for the navy or aircraft?

Activity: 'Top Trumps'

Draw up a set of 'Top Trump' cards for the competing great powers of Europe in the 1920s. You could include each country's flag or a national emblem to add colour. You will need to rate each country's potential in the following categories: population; production; economy; army; navy; empire.

Use your cards to help you write a summary of the relative strengths of the competing nations and why Italy needed German support to take on Britain and France.

Chapter 10 **Italy 1934–38: A great power?**

Key questions

- Did Italian foreign policy fundamentally change in these years?
- What did the war in East Africa signify of Italy's desires and capabilities?
- Why and with what consequences did Italy become involved in the Spanish Civil War?
- In what ways were Mussolini's foreign policy initiatives in these years successes or failures?

Many textbooks contrast Mussolini's behaviour in the period after 1934 with the first ten years of his rule. In the earlier period, it is said, we have a cautious *Duce* co-operating with Britain and France and promoting harmony. After 1934 we have a strutting warmonger building his empire and asserting Italy as a great power. Increasingly the partner is Nazi Germany and the enemy Britain. It is said that changed circumstances can explain this shift in Mussolini's behaviour and the assumption is that Mussolini was merely an opportunist responding to these circumstances. As indicated in the last chapter, this is not the position taken here. Mussolini was a strutting warmonger from the start. It was merely that he was previously constrained by circumstances and therefore unable to act freely.

Take note

Draw up a list of Mussolini's aims in this period. As you work through this section, make notes around each of the events and how they helped or hindered these aims.

Timeline

June 1934	Hitler and Mussolini met for first time in Venice
July 1934	Italian confrontation with Germany over Austria
April 1935	Stresa Conference
October 1935	Outbreak of war in Abyssinia
November 1935	League voted to apply sanctions to Italy
December 1935	Hoare–Laval Pact; Hoare–Laval Pact dropped; Britain backed League of Nations to confront Italy; Hoare replaced by Anthony Eden, seen as much more anti-Italian
June 1936	Ciano made foreign minister
July 1936	Outbreak of Spanish Civil War
November 1936	Rome–Berlin Axis announced
March 1937	Battle of Guadalajara: Italian troops suffer defeat in Spain
September 1937	Mussolini visited Germany
November 1937	Italy joined Japan and Germany in Anti-Comintern Pact
March 1938	Germany occupied Austria
May 1938	State visit of Hitler to Italy
September 1938	Munich Conference

How far did Italian foreign policy change?

Circumstances did change in the 1930s and, like any good politician, Mussolini took advantage. These changes enabled him to do what he had always wanted to do; his aims remained the same but the opportunities increased. Britain was weakened by the economic slump and increasingly absorbed in the problems of recovery. Britain's defence spending reached its lowest level in 1933.

Hitler's coming to power the same year was the nationalist triumph in Germany that Mussolini had long hoped for and predicted. Now Germany would rearm and confront France, and possibly Britain, giving Mussolini his ally and making the seizure of the Mediterranean possible. Even in the 1920s, Mussolini had made secret contacts with the German army and toyed with the idea of an alliance, but Weimar Germany was too weak to act.

However, Hitler's appointment as chancellor of Germany did not initially produce the chain of events that Mussolini hoped for. In fact, circumstances forced him into an unwanted confrontation. Mussolini had already made it quite clear that he was prepared to sacrifice the **Austrian buffer state** in return for a German alliance. He had hinted at this to the Hungarians, who became his allies in 1927, and told Grandi clearly in March 1933. However, any change to Austria's status would have to be part of a deal with Italy and not a threatening military seizure. The king, the army and the diplomats in the Italian Foreign Office would not accept German troops forcibly occupying Austria and bringing Germany to Italy's frontier. With such a powerful neighbour, all Italy's gains in 1919 would be put at risk. Italian public opinion was also not prepared for such a move by Germany. As a result, in July 1934, when Austrian Nazis (with Berlin's blessing) killed the Austrian chancellor, Dollfuss, an ally and friend of Mussolini, the *Duce* had to respond. Italian troops were rushed to the Brenner Pass and Hitler was forced to announce that the actions in Vienna had nothing to do with him and Austria was still independent of Germany. Events were forcing Mussolini in the opposite direction than he wished to move, towards hostility to Nazi Germany and greater dependence on Britain and France.

Another event accidentally drove Italy closer to France, though quite unexpectedly. In 1934, Italian military intelligence engineered the assassination of the king of Yugoslavia in Marseilles by Croat terrorists. The French foreign minister, Louis Barthou, was an incidental victim and his replacement, Pierre Laval, proved very anxious to improve relations with Italy. He secretly gave his blessing to Italian aggression in East Africa in a meeting with Mussolini in Rome in January 1935. The improvement of relations with France had the advantage of raising Italy's value with the Germans, who next time would be more circumspect with Austria and not simply try to launch a smash and grab raid. The culmination of this period of co-operation was a conference in April, at the Italian town of **Stresa**, when Mussolini, Laval and the British prime minister, Ramsey MacDonald, met to condemn open German rearmament.

War and empire, 1935–36

The 1930s was marked by a cult of empire and the heritage of ancient Rome. Triumphal Roman-style arches were erected to decorate Italian cities and remind Italians that they were the heirs of greatness. A series of colourful events were organised to celebrate the 2000-year anniversary of great Romans: the poets Virgil in 1930, Horace in 1935 and, greatest of all, Augustus, the first emperor, in 1937.

Glossary

Austrian buffer state

Many Italians were anxious to have a weak state on their northern border rather than a powerful and potentially threatening Germany. Austria was useful as such a friendly buffer state separating Italy from Germany.

The Stresa Conference

The Stresa conference was the last time that Italy really appeared to co-operate with the Western powers against Germany. It established what was grandly called the 'Stresa Front', which stood against any future violations of the Treaty of Versailles by Germany. In reality it meant little. Britain refused to give the agreement real teeth and, shortly afterwards, negotiated a deal with Germany, breaking the naval clauses of Versailles. Each power pursued its own interests and, by the end of 1935, the Stresa Front had disintegrated.

Take note

How did changing circumstances drive a wedge between Italy and the Western powers? What were the results of the Italian involvement in Abyssinia and in Spain?

Three Ethiopians salute an image of Mussolini, Abyssina 1936 (note the fasces to either side)

Abyssinia: The popular war

Abyssinia was to be the basis of the new Roman Empire. The desire for revenge for the humiliation at Adowa in 1896 was widespread and Mussolini shared the sentiment. He had ordered general planning for a war of conquest in 1926 and detailed planning began in 1932. Now that France seemed to have given its approval there was nothing really standing in the way. Huge numbers of troops were concentrated on the frontier. Initial planning indicated that three divisions would be sufficient against a largely under-equipped enemy lacking artillery, machine guns and an air force. Mussolini was determined to have no repetition of the 1896 fiasco. He told the army to use ten divisions, supported by 450 planes. On 2 Oct 1935, the war for revenge and empire began.

Haile Selassie, the Abyssinian emperor, appealed to the League of Nations for help and the League condemned Italy and voted for sanctions. Mussolini urged his army to press on at all speed and use whatever weapons were necessary to secure a rapid victory. Chemical weapons were employed, causing horrific injuries to unprotected Abyssinian soldiers and civilians. Mustard gas was dropped, both by bombs and by spraying, and shells filled with arsine (a compound made from arsenic) poisoned wells and water supplies for both humans and animals.

Britain and France were embarrassed. They did not wish to drive Italy into the arms of Hitler, but public opinion, particularly in Britain, was outraged by Mussolini's behaviour and wanted the invasion stopped. The British foreign secretary, Sir Samuel Hoare, and Pierre Laval met in Paris and proposed a compromise deal by which Italy would be given a large part of Abyssinia. The deal became known as the Hoare–Laval pact. Before Italy had a chance to reject it, the deal was leaked to the press and outrage in Britain forced the government to repudiate Hoare, who resigned. It reputedly produced one of King George V's only jokes – 'No more Hoares to Paris then'.

The new British foreign secretary, Sir Anthony Eden, took a tougher line and backed sanctions against Italy. The British fleet in the Mediterranean was reinforced. The extensive restrictions on trade hit the Italian economy hard. Britain could have forced Italian compliance with the League by closing the Suez Canal to Italian ships, which would have blocked their access to Abyssinia, forcing them to sail all the way round Africa instead. However, Britain thought that this would amount to a declaration of war on Italy. In addition, despite the build-up of British naval power in the Mediterranean, the fleet was short of ammunition and anti-aircraft guns. Mussolini knew the British did not want to fight as the Italian secret service had a spy in the British embassy and were reading top secret British diplomatic documents. He decided he could bluff it out and defy them.

The war was massively popular in Italy amongst all sections of the population. The king was thrilled to be made Emperor of Abyssinia. Women queued to give up their wedding rings for gold to help beat the sanctions. Even southern peasants reacted favourably to rumours of jobs and land for the taking. The Church gave its blessing. It really did look as though, in addition to avenging Adowa, Mussolini had united Italy in a nationalist frenzy as never before. This is what fascism was all about. On 5 May 1936, Italian troops entered Addis Ababa and Haile Selassie fled. It was Mussolini's finest hour, or at least it seemed to be, as his popularity peaked.

A diplomatic turnaround accompanied the war. Germany, who had initially supplied 10,000 rifles to Abyssinia, now helped Italy to beat the sanctions. Two-thirds of Italy's coal imports, vital for her steel industry, were supplied by Germany. Mussolini responded by letting Hitler know in January 1936 that he no longer saw Austria as a problem and invited Germany to enlarge its influence there. In February, Hitler informed Italy that Germany was likely to violate Locarno and reoccupy the Rhineland with troops. Mussolini signalled his approval. When Hitler carried out his threat in March, and the League voted for sanctions, Italy refused to join in. The anti-Nazi Italian ambassador in Berlin, Vittorio Cerruti, whose wife was Jewish, had already been moved from Berlin to Paris in 1935 and now other senior anti-Nazi diplomatic officials were sacked and replaced. Mussolini appointed his own son-in-law, the pro-Nazi **Count Galeazzo Ciano**, as foreign minister in the summer of 1936. In October he sacked the **under-secretary of war** and replaced him with a more pro-Nazi general. The culmination of this process was the signing of the **Axis agreement** between Rome and Berlin on 1 November 1936. It is important to realise that this aligning with Germany was not forced on Mussolini by circumstances but circumstances now allowed him to do what he had always wanted to. Basking in the glory of the Abyssinian triumph, the king, the army and the traditional diplomatic elite in the Foreign Office could not stop him.

Count Ciano in 1939, inspecting a German guard of honour

The cost of the war to Italy was horrendous, but at the time few bothered to calculate it. 600,000 Italian troops had been sent to Abyssinia. Nearly 12,000 died and 200,000 were wounded, injured or fell seriously sick. A quarter of a million Abyssinian soldiers and civilians died. The war cost eight times what it had been estimated to do. 4.2 million shells had been fired and 29,000 vehicles deployed. 39 billion lire was the final price of the new empire. The war did not end in 1936 either as, encouraged by French money and weapons, guerrilla warfare occupied thousands of Italian troops until 1939. In the spring of 1941 the whole empire was overrun rapidly by British troops and Haile Selassie was restored to his throne.

Biography

Count Galeazzo Ciano

1903–1944

The son of a senior naval officer, Ciano married Mussolini's daughter Edda. He served as press and propaganda minister and then as a bomber pilot in the Abyssinian War. He was appointed foreign minister to push for closer relations with Germany. However, he became disillusioned with Germany, in particular with the bombastic German foreign minister Von Ribbentrop, and began to press for a rapprochement with the Western Allies in 1939. He took part in the coup against his father-in-law in 1943. The Germans never forgave him and insisted on his execution in 1944.

Glossary

Under-secretary of war

Second to the Minister of War and therefore the effective head of the War Ministry, as Mussolini took the title of minister himself.

Axis agreement

This was a loose agreement to co-operate and co-ordinate policy, not a full-blown military alliance. The two powers agreed that Europe would turn on decisions made in Berlin and Rome, like the Earth does on its axis. The two became known in the war years as the Axis Powers.

Italian involvement in Spain

In the first three months of the war, Italy provided General Franco and the Nationalists with 130 aircraft, 2500 tons of bombs, 500 cannon, 700 mortars, 12,000 machine guns and almost 4000 vehicles. The war lasted until April 1939.

On the other side, the Republicans were aided by the presence of several 'International Brigades' of volunteers from across Europe and the USA. 3350 volunteers came from Italy and 3000 from Germany to continue the fight against fascism.

The Battle of Guadalajara

Italian commanders tried to show their military superiority by acting independently of the Spanish Nationalist Army during the Battle of Guadalajara. However, it was a disaster. Supply problems meant that their tanks were left stranded, they had no air cover and those tanks that could move were outclassed by superior Russian tanks. The Italian commanders had no maps and their soldiers were dressed for tropical weather during a harsh Spanish winter. The Italians were trounced, and Mussolini proclaimed that no Italian solider would be allowed back home until the war was won.

Spain: The unpopular war

No sooner had victory been declared in East Africa than Mussolini was engaged in another conflict. A civil war broke out in Spain in July 1936 when the Spanish army launched a coup to topple the Republican government in Madrid. Mussolini expressed support for the rebels and sent a few tanks and planes initially. In December the decision was taken for much greater intervention and around 50,000 Italian 'volunteers' from the army and the Fascist militia were dispatched to Spain to help the forces of General Franco against the Republic, itself increasingly dependent on aid from communist Russia. Hitler dispatched a major air contingent which became known as the Condor Legion and thus Rome and Berlin finally found themselves fighting as allies.

Mussolini's motives were mixed.

- First, there was an element of anti-communism. This was popular with the Catholic Church, which regarded the Republican extremists in Spain with horror, as churches were burnt and rumours of the rape of nuns spread.

- Second, there was certainly a satisfaction in co-operating with Nazi Germany, the new Axis partner.

- Third, and more important still, was the desire to use war as a training ground for the new Fascist Italy. It was necessary to harden the soft Italians and only a succession of wars could do this.

- Intervention also emphasised Italian greatness. Italy was determining great events in the west Mediterranean and spreading its influence.

The results of intervention were not what Mussolini desired, although Franco was eventually triumphant. Far from enhancing Italian prestige, Italian troops suffered a humiliating defeat at the **Battle of Guadalajara** in March 1937. 400 Italians died and even more were taken prisoner. In part, the defeat was at the hands of Italian 'red' volunteers fighting on the other side. Mussolini was later to order that any Italians captured volunteering for the opposing Republicans were to be executed. The war was not popular in Italy as it cost a lot of money and seemed pointless to most Italians.

The cost was terrible. Huge amounts of equipment were sent, including artillery, tanks and transport. It has been estimated that the Italian army in 1940 could have been double the strength that it was if so much had not been sent to Spain. Possibly an additional four or five motorised divisions could have been equipped and this might have altered the strategic balance in North Africa in Italy's favour in 1940–41. There was a huge increase in defence spending between 1934 and 1939, as the table below makes clear, but most of the increased money was absorbed by the wars in Abyssinia and Spain.

The diplomatic results were also in some ways unfavourable to Italy. Tensions were increased with Britain and France – who accelerated their own rearmament. Italian submarines tried to torpedo traffic to Republican ports and also attacked a British destroyer, possibly by accident. The track record of the Italian submarine service was not great and HMS *Havock* survived, as did 20 of the 24 cargo ships the Italian submarines tried to sink. As relations with the Western powers deteriorated, so Italy's dependence on Germany increased. Mussolini carried out a state visit to Germany in September 1937 and was impressed by increasing German might. In November, he joined the **Anti-Comintern Pact**, linking Italy, Germany and Japan in a grouping aimed on the surface at the Soviet Union but, in many ways, at British interests too. In March 1938, Hitler invaded and annexed Austria, bringing the Third Reich to the Italian border. Hitler claimed that he would never forget Mussolini's acceptance of this. In reality, however, Mussolini was now tied to Germany as the junior partner. At the **Munich Conference** in September, Mussolini promoted peace because Italy was not ready for war, but in every way he championed Germany's interests.

Year	Army	Air Force	Navy
1934–35	2639	810	310
1935–36	7093	2241	2850
1936–37	9050	3628	3423
1937–38	5794	3923	2970
1938–39	6685	4296	3429

Italian defence spending (million lire)

Conclusion: Was Mussolini's foreign policy a success or a failure in 1934–38?

Italy appeared to have acted in these years as a great power and this brought Mussolini considerable prestige at home and abroad. Even at the Munich Conference in 1938, where he was not the main player, he appeared to be one of the big four, courted by all the other great powers. Mussolini had defied the League of Nations and expanded the empire in Africa. He had also established close relations with Germany, a long-term aim and an essential precondition of challenging British domination of the Mediterranean. Despite the setbacks and cost of the war in Spain, the side he backed eventually won in 1939 and he appeared to have gained a friendly client state in Franco's government.

On the negative side, Italy had been bled white and her military strength sapped. Austria had become German and there could be little doubt that Italy was the junior partner in the Axis. The increasingly close relationship with Germany was not popular with Italians at large, or with the king or the pope. The anti-Semitic laws introduced in 1938 to bring Italy into line with German beliefs and practices were not popular in Italy and the increasingly anti-British stance was not popular with the elites. Unless major gains could come from the arrangement, Mussolini's pro-German policy was likely to undermine his own power in Italy.

Activity: Italian priorities

Use the table on defence spending to work out the changing priorities of Italian foreign policy during this period.

Activity: Italian progress

Compare Italy's strengths in the 1920s versus the 1930s.
- How prepared for war against the great powers of Britain and France was Italy by 1938?
- Had Mussolini's policies helped or hindered Italian progress?

Anti-Comintern Pact

The Comintern was the Communist International based in Moscow and devoted to the spread of communism worldwide. The Anti-Comitern Pact was theoretically aimed against the spread of communism. In reality it was largely an anti-British grouping.

Munich Conference

Major diplomatic meeting held on 29 September 1938 to settle German claims on Czechoslovakia. Neville Chamberlain, the British prime minister, had appealed to Mussolini to encourage Hitler to avoid war and to negotiate.

Taking it further

Foreign intervention played a key part in the Spanish Civil War. Compare the levels of support provided by Mussolini and Hitler, and the relative impacts the two nations had on the outcome of the war. There is a chapter on foreign involvement in the war in Edexcel's *Republicanism, Civil War and Francoism in Spain, 1931–75* (chapter 7).

Chapter 11 Hitler's sidekick: Italy 1939–43 'The tale of a punctured chin'

Key questions

- Why did Mussolini sign the Pact of Steel?
- Why did Mussolini wait until 1940 to join the war?
- Why did Italy suffer such a series of military defeats?

At Munich, Mussolini was hailed as a peacemaker and it was as such that he was greeted on his return to Italy. In reality, Munich stirred up his determination for fresh aggression. He felt contempt for Britain and France, and renewed admiration and envy for the militaristic Nazi Germany. He talked of an aggressive alliance with Germany and Japan, not just an Anti-Comintern Pact: 'We want an alliance to change the map of the world.' There was a new tone of aggression towards France, with the Italian Chamber of Deputies raising demands for Tunis, Corsica, Nice and Savoy to be given to Italy in November 1938. A visit by the British prime minister, Neville Chamberlain, to Rome in January 1939 is often hailed as a sign of Mussolini dithering as to his future course. In reality it reflected Chamberlain's near-hopeless aim to detach Mussolini from Hitler, or at least to use him as a moderating force. Mussolini was far from being that and his private comments after the meeting emphasise the contempt he felt for bourgeois politicians like Chamberlain who talked of peace and carried an umbrella. They were simply 'the tired sons of rich men who will lose an empire'.

Take note

As you read through this chapter, think about the reasons why Mussolini held back in 1939 and finally committed to war in 1940. Make notes linking to these reasons, explaining why Italy's performance in the war was so disastrous. What went wrong?

Timeline

April 1939	Italy annexed Albania
May 1939	Pact of Steel
September 1939	Outbreak of war – Italy stayed neutral
June 1940	Italy declared war on France and Britain
August 1940	Italy conquered British Somaliland
September 1940	Italy invaded Egypt
October 1940	Italy invaded Greece
November 1940	British inflicted heavy damage on Italian fleet at Taranto
December 1940	Devastating British counter-offensive in Egypt began
February 1941	Trapped Italian army in Libya surrendered
March 1941	Battle of Matapan – Italian cruisers sunk; British re-conquered Somaliland
April 1941	British destroyed Italian armies in Ethiopia
October 1942	El Alamein – Italian-German armies defeated in Egypt
May 1943	All German and Italian forces in North Africa surrendered
July 1943	Anglo-American invasion of Sicily, Mussolini deposed
Sept 1943	Allied invasion of Italy
Oct 1943	New Italian government declared war on Germany

Following in Germany's wake, 1938–39

Mussolini was somewhat taken aback by Germany's next move, in March 1939. Hitler broke the Munich Agreement and occupied the rest of Czechoslovakia, guaranteed by all four great powers in the previous September's meeting. Mussolini was not overcome with moral outrage but with surprise and envy. He felt that Italy had to engage in a similar dramatic gesture and, in April, Italian troops invaded Albania and annexed it. Ciano had bribed the important power-brokers in this backward Balkan state and there was no resistance. In

'Sad Tale of a Punctured Chin' by Low, *Evening Standard* 25 November 1940

May Mussolini got his offensive alliance with Germany, generally known as the Pact of Steel. Mussolini had wanted it named the Pact of Blood! Ciano, who negotiated it with some personal hesitations, thought that he had an undertaking that war would be avoided until 1942 or 1943, when Italy would be ready. Ciano, like the king, the army chiefs and many of the old elite, was unhappy at the mad rush to aggression. They would have preferred Italy to move towards more friendly relations with Britain and France. Mussolini would have none of this, however.

By August 1939 it was increasingly obvious that Germany was going to attack Poland, with the risk of a general European war following. Mussolini's initial response was to take the opportunity to attack Greece and Yugoslavia. The king made it completely clear to his prime minister that the army was in no shape to fight and this was clearly the case. On 25 August Mussolini had the humiliating task of informing Hitler that, in the event of war, Italy could not honour the Pact of Steel unless Germany could meet a long list of Italian economic demands. Mussolini knew that these could not be met. Economic realities, the debilitating effects of two wars in the 1930s, and pressure from the king and the old elites, all ensured Italy's neutrality, at least in the short-term.

Why war came in June 1940

In June 1940, Mussolini reversed his decision of the previous August and joined in the Second World War. The reasons for this reversal are many. His son-in-law, the foreign minister, and the king both opposed entry but this time Mussolini got his way. As early as 1 February, Ciano was recording in his diary that 'His will is fixed and decided on war.' In March, Germany promised to make up the shortfall in coal that would result from a British blockade by sending 12 million tons annually by rail. The really decisive change, however, was the rapid collapse of France in May and June 1940.

This destroyed the massive Allied naval supremacy in the Mediterranean and, although the British fleet was still formidable, the British navy would be stretched coping with both Germany and Italy. The rich pickings on offer were just too tempting. France seemed on her last legs and, if Italy was going to make gains, then some Italians would have to be in at the kill. Mussolini could bring 22 divisions to bear on the six French divisions holding the alpine front. Britain seemed horribly vulnerable with just over 36,000 under-equipped troops in Egypt compared to over 200,000 Italians in Libya. Italy could muster 425 aircraft against 205 British planes. In East Africa, British colonies were defended by a few thousand against a massive force of over 250,000 Italians in Ethiopia.

On 10 June, Italy declared war on Britain and France. This time Italy would show the world!

Defeat and humiliation

The assault on the French alpine front by overwhelming numbers of Italians produced only stalemate – and heavy losses compared to those inflicted on the French. The Italian troops were poorly equipped and under-trained: 632 Italians died and 2631 were wounded, compared to 37 Frenchmen killed and 42 wounded. It was not a good beginning but, mercifully for Mussolini, the fighting was short-lived. Two weeks after Italy declared war, the fighting ceased. France, which had been totally out-manoeuvred by a bold German thrust where it was not expected, surrendered to Germany on 22 June and reluctantly concluded an armistice with the Italians two days later.

The invasion of Egypt, September 1940

Despite the doubts of Marshall Graziani, Mussolini ordered the invasion of Egypt in September 1940. The Italians outnumbered the British forces by more than six to one, but were widely spread and their leaders reluctant. They were only too aware of the inadequacy of the forces available.
One officer wrote 'We're trying to fight this... as though it were a colonial war... We are not fighting the Ethiopians now.' The invasion stalled as Graziani dug in to prepare to resist the expected British counter-attack.

Italian military operations on the Alpine Front

The war against Britain started in a slightly more promising fashion. The Duke of Aosta invaded British Somaliland with overwhelming force and the Royal Navy withdrew the small garrison in an orderly fashion. In Libya, the Italian commander-in-chief was shot down by his own anti-aircraft guns but his replacement, Marshal Graziani, began a slow **invasion of British Egypt**. They reached Sidi Barrani, around 60 miles over the frontier, and halted on 18 September. The town was of little significance, containing only one small shop and two brothels, but the Italian army made little further progress.

Mussolini's attention shifted to a new theatre of operations in October. Hitler, without prior warning, had moved German forces into Romania, mainly to head off Russian incursions. Italy believed that they had influence there and the *Duce* was affronted. He and Ciano hatched what they hoped would be an equally bold gesture for Italy. They would invade Greece. It turned into a disaster. The Greeks held the Italians and then counter-attacked, invading Albania. Disaster also struck the main Italian fleet in **Taranto** when the British launched an airborne attack from a single aircraft carrier in November. Half the Italian battle fleet was put out of action. In December, a small British army in Egypt counter-attacked Graziani's force. By February 130,000 Italians had been captured, along with 400 tanks and 850 guns. Britain occupied all of eastern Libya for minimal loss. Between February and May 1941, the Italian East African empire was conquered. The whole Fascist empire had come tumbling down in a matter of months.

Only massive German intervention now gave Italy hope. The Germans invaded Greece and occupied Athens. A small but efficient German army under General Rommel arrived in North Africa to bolster the remaining Italians. This efficient force, named the Afrika Korps, kept the war going until May 1943, when the British (with American help) finally gained control of the whole of North Africa. Only the presence of the German air force stopped the Royal Navy having full control of the Mediterranean. Italy was increasingly a poor relation of Germany. The war had proved a disaster and the culmination of Mussolini's foreign policy, far from proving Italy a great power, had brought suffering and humiliation.

In the summer of 1943, Sicily was invaded and conquered by an Anglo-American army. In September, mainland Italy was invaded and the island of Sardinia was taken. Mussolini, partially broken and dispirited, was deposed by the Fascist Grand Council in July and imprisoned by royal command. The new government announced an armistice on 8 September.

Explaining defeat

The root of Italy's problems lay in the backward nature of the Italian economy. Italy simply could not produce enough equipment and machinery to supply modern fighting forces. Individual weapons or planes might show design genius but overall Italy could not compete with the big boys, as Mussolini so desperately wished to do.

> ### The Battle of Taranto, November 1940
>
> Originally planned using two aircraft carriers, the Royal Navy were forced to put 'Operation Judgment' into action using just HMS *Illustrious*. For the loss of only two aircraft, the *Illustrious'* strike force took three Italian battleships and a heavy cruiser out of action – demonstrating the importance of carriers (which the Italians lacked) in naval warfare. The Japanese studied the British tactics at Taranto for their later attack on Pearl Harbour.

	1938
Britain	181
Germany	214
France	74
USA	528
Italy	46

Total industrial potential (index)

	1938
Britain	10.7
Germany	12.7
France	4.4
Italy	2.2

Share of world manufacturing (index)

	1939
Britain	7940
France	3163
Germany	8295
Italy	c.2000

Aircraft production

Italian FIAT CR42 bi plane, no match for the single-wing Spitfire

	Battleships	Aircraft carriers	Cruisers	Destroyers	Submarines
Britain	15	7	64	184	58
France	10	1	50	28	71
Germany	2	0	8	22	57
Italy	4	0	15	59	105

Naval capabilities, 1939

- Italian aircraft were not only produced in too small a number but they lacked quality. Italy's basic fighter, the FIAT CR42 was a superb biplane but no match for the single-wing Hurricane, let alone the Spitfire, which was nearly 150 kph faster. They had no long-range bombers capable of reaching Gibraltar or Alexandria and most Italian planes lacked radios.

- Italian tanks were light and virtually obsolete, dismissed as tin cans by both their occupants and the British. Marshall Balbo commented: 'Our light tanks, already old and armed only with machine guns, are completely out-classed. The machine guns of the British... easily pierce their armour.'

- The ships of the Italian navy looked attractive and tended to be speedy, but they were thinly armoured and lacked radar. Italy had built no aircraft carriers. Her navy had been designed primarily to re-fight the First World War.

The military organisation of Italy mirrored its technical inferiority. The army was bedevilled by promotion according to seniority, which meant that people who had served the longest were promoted ahead of those who were the most talented. There was little interest in innovation and even less in co-operation with the air force. There was in fact minimal cross-service planning despite the fact that Mussolini doubled as minister for all three armed services. Each jealously guarded their independence and Mussolini showed no interest or aptitude for enforcing co-operation. In fact, as minister he was more interested in prestige and the trivial, such as smart marching, than showing a real grasp of what mattered. He had none of Hitler's interest in the nitty-gritty of warfare or his grasp of strategy. As a good journalist, Mussolini was fascinated by presentation. He tended to mistake appearance for reality. The dramatic gesture always had priority. In declaring war on 10 June 1940, nobody thought to give warning to Italy's merchant navy, a large part of which was simply taken over by the British in the ports which they controlled. It was to be symptomatic of the conduct of the war. In a very crucial sense it was symptomatic of the whole history of the regime.

The last phase, September 1943–April 1945

On 12 September 1943, a daring German commando raid rescued Mussolini from his prison. German troops poured into Italy through the alpine railways, which the new pro-Allied government had failed to block. They seized Rome before the Allies could reach it and ensured that there would be a long, hard slog up the peninsula.

Before the Germans could seize them, the king, his family and the new government fled south to the Allies. There were now two Italys, one in the south under British and American occupation and a northern Fascist state with Mussolini as a puppet ruler, but in reality under the German army and Albert Kesselring, the German commander. Slowly, and with considerable casualties, the Allies clawed their way north. Rome was captured in June 1944. There was bitter fighting between the Germans and partisans, who were Italian opponents of fascism. Thousands of partisans and innocent civilians were killed in reprisals by the German army. By 1945 the Allied armies had reached the plains of northern Italy. The war was clearly lost for Mussolini's Fascists. In April Mussolini and his mistress, Clara Petacci, were caught by partisans near to Lake Como and shot. Their bodies were later strung up by their feet and tied to the gantry of a nearby petrol station. The chin no longer jutted out in arrogant assertion of its owner's power and Italy's greatness. The voice was at long last silent.

Conclusion: Why was Mussolini's chin 'punctured'?

Mussolini's dream of national greatness had ended in appalling suffering for the Italian people. Their country had been fought over so often in past centuries and Italy had achieved nothing but national humiliation. For nearly two decades, Mussolini had cleverly given the illusion of power and provided the Italian people with solid gains in terms of stability and some economic advances. Briefly in the mid-1930s it appeared that he had succeeded in making Italy 'great, respected and feared'. Italy and its *Duce* had been courted by all the other great powers of Europe. But he tied himself increasingly to Hitler and the Third Reich. The connection had proved toxic. It was a fatal embrace.

Activity: Playing general

Try to work out a winning strategy for Italy in 1940. Clue – don't try to do too many things and play to Italy's strengths, not those of her opponents.

Could Mussolini's Italy have come out on top?

Write a letter to Mussolini as his chief general in the winter of 1939, either urging for war or peace, explaining your views and strategies.

> **Taking it further**
>
> Research in detail some of the crucial defeats suffered by Italy in the Second World War. Why did they lose each one and what were the consequences?
> - The battle of Taranto 1940
> - The battle of Cape Matapan 1941
> - The failure to conquer Greece 1940
> - The defeat in Libya by Britain 1940–41

Skills Builder 4: **Extended writing**

So far, in the Skills Builders, you have learned about:

- the importance of writing in paragraphs
- answering questions on causation and change
- how to write introductions and conclusions.

Now you are going to learn about how to write a full response to an examination question. Remember you will only have 40 minutes for each answer so you need to make the most of your time.

Read the QUESTION PAPER thoroughly

You will have a choice of two questions on this topic, but you only need to answer one. Make sure that you make the right choice. Don't rush. Allow time – a few minutes – to decide which question to answer. You won't have time to change your mind halfway through the exam.

Read YOUR CHOSEN QUESTION thoroughly

Once you have made your choice, examine the question and work out what you are expected to do.

What is the question asking you to do?

There are a number of different types of question you could be asked. Examples are:

- How far?
- How important?
- How extensive?
- To what extent?
- Why?

Make sure that your answer is relevant to the type of question that has been asked.

In the first four question types, you will be expected to assess a range of factors. You will weigh up the importance of each factor you mention in relation to the question. You will need to reach a judgment on the question in hand. For instance:

> (A) 'Mussolini allied with Germany because a common ideology drove him into the alliance.' How far do you agree with this opinion?

In answering this question you will be expected to provide reasons for the development of the Italian–German alliance. You will also be expected to assess the importance of the stated factor, i.e. ideology, as opposed to others, such as circumstances, producing clashes with Britain and France.

Make sure you cover the whole question

Here is an example:

> (B) How far did Mussolini succeed in making Italy a great power in the years 1922–40?

In this question you must make sure that you explain both aspects of the question:

- the definition of Italy as a great power
- the issue of success, which needs criteria.

Make a plan

Once you are clear about what the question is asking, sketch out what you intend to cover. Write down what you think will be relevant information in the form of a list or a concept map. Then organise your information in a way which best answers the question.

Writing the answer

Make sure that you:

- write a brief introduction, setting out your argument and what you will be discussing in your answer
- write a separate paragraph for each factor/reason you give. In the paragraph, make sure that you make a clear point and support it with specific examples
- make a clear link at the end of each paragraph between the point you have made and the question, showing how the point answers the question
- avoid just writing descriptions
- avoid merely 'telling a story'
- write a concluding paragraph which sums up your arguments and provides a clear judgment on the question.

Pace yourself

Success in an examination is based partly on effective time management. If you have approximately 40 minutes to answer a question, make sure that after about 12 or 13 minutes you have written about one-third of your answer. And after 35 minutes you should be thinking about and then writing your conclusion.

If you run short of time, make sure that you can still write a proper concluding paragraph. If necessary, you can save time by cutting short your treatment of the paragraph or paragraphs before, by:

- writing the first sentence containing your point
- bullet-pointing your evidence for this point – the information that backs it up
- writing the last sentence of the paragraph which explains the link between your point and the question.

EXAM SUCCESS!

- Read the question paper thoroughly.
- Timing: pace yourself.
- Be clear about the focus of the question you have chosen.
- Make a brief plan of your answer before starting writing.

Activity: Write your own introduction

Write an introduction to the following question:

> (C) How far do you agree that Mussolini's regime was brutal in dealing with its opponents?

You will need to draw on your knowledge of the repressive nature of the regime and the work of OVRA and the Special Tribunal. You may also wish to introduce examples from outside Italy, i.e. the repression in North Africa and Ethiopia which, in some ways, stands in sharp contrast to the conduct of the regime within Italy.

Activity: Write your own conclusion

Using Question (C) above, write a conclusion of not more than four sentences. Try to write it in five minutes.

Activity: Write an introduction and conclusion

Here is another example of a question:

> (D) How far do you agree that the Fascist regime improved Italians' living standards in the years 1925–39?

Now write an introduction and a conclusion – each in approximately five minutes.

Tip – plan the conclusion first. You will always find it easier to write an introduction once you have decided what your conclusion will be. This is because, once you know where your answer is going, you can introduce it.

Activity: Write your own answer

Now write your own answer to this question, following the guidance given above:

> (E) How far do you agree that Italy's economic weakness prevented Mussolini from launching a major war before 1940?

Examzone

Now that you have finished the course content, you will have to do the last bits of preparation for the exam itself. This advice covers two important elements for exam success: revising the information and using your information well in the examination.

This topic – 'The Collapse of the Liberal State and the Triumph of Fascism in Italy, 1896–1943' – is part of Edexcel's Option E/F: The Expansion and Challenge of Nationalism, in Unit 1. The Unit 1 exam will be 1 hour and 20 minutes in length, and is worth 60 marks in total.

In the exam you will be given the choice of two questions on the topic, 'The Collapse of the Liberal State and the Triumph of Fascism in Italy, 1896–1943'. You will be expected to answer one of these and should spend no more than half the examination time answering it. You will also have to answer another question from a different topic. You will be expected to answer the questions you choose in essay form.

What to expect

You will need to remember information, but the exam is mainly testing whether or not you can apply the relevant information in answering a question. You will be assessed on your ability to recall and select historical knowledge and to deploy it (i.e. make use of knowledge to support your points). You can see that it's not just knowing what happened which counts, but understanding how to use what you know.

You will also be assessed on your ability to present historical explanations that show an understanding of history. You should read the question carefully to make sure you answer it in the right way. Sometimes questions will simply begin 'Why'. These are asking you to analyse the causes of an event or development. For the highest marks you will need to show how factors combined to bring about the event.

Most questions will ask you for a judgment. Here are some different types of question stems you may come across in the exam:

1. How far was x responsible for y?
2. To what extent did x change?
3. How far did x depend on y?
4. Did x play a major part in y?

Although judgment questions come in a variety of forms, they are all asking you to balance points. In the case of example 2 below, you will be looking for evidence of change and of continuity in order to reach a judgment about the extent of change.

When you choose your question in the examination, take note of what sort of judgment it asks you to make. The essay questions test a variety of skills. Here are some examples of different skills being tested by the questions.

1. The analysis of, and judgment about, the **key features** of a situation.
   For example: *To what extent did Mussolini's dictatorship rely on repression in the years 1925–43?*

2. The analysis of, and judgment about, the extent of **change**.
   For example: *How far do you agree that Mussolini improved Italy's international position in the years 1922–40?*

3. The analysis of **consequences** or **effects**.
   For example: *How accurate is it to say that fear of socialism was the key factor determining the rise of fascism in the years 1919–22?*

4. The analysis of, and judgment about, the **causes** of a historical event or situation.
   For example: *How far were political divisions responsible for the weakness of the Liberal state in the years 1896–1914?*

Another type of question will ask you how far you agree with a statement. This is still a judgment question. You should clarify what the statement is about so that you know what the question expects of you:

- Is it a statement about causation, like this question: *How far do you agree that Mussolini's appointment as prime minister in 1922 was due to the support of the traditional elites?*

- Or is it about change, like this question: *How far do you agree that the Fascist regime's economic policies failed to improve the living standards of the Italian people in the years 1925–43?*

When you are clear about what the question wants from you, you can use what you have learned in the Skills Builder sections of this book to produce an answer based on extended writing (an essay), which will help you to gain high marks.

How to revise

Make a revision plan

Before you start revising, make a plan. Otherwise it is easy to waste your precious revision time. It is helpful to look at your exam dates and work backwards to the first date you intend to start revising. Here are some tips on how to create a revision plan:

1. First, fill in the dates of your examinations and then any regular commitments you have. This will help give you a realistic idea of how much time you have to revise.

2. Plan your time carefully, assigning more time to topics you find difficult.

3. Use a revision 'checklist'. Look at what you need to know and try to identify any gaps in your knowledge.

4. Now fill in the timetable with sensible work slots and breaks.

5. Keep to this timetable! Organise yourself well and it will help you to fulfil your potential. If you have not prepared a revision plan yet, it is not too late to start. Put your plan up somewhere visible so you can refer back to it.

Revision tips

- Revise often – try to do a little every day.

- Make sure you have one day a week when you don't do revision or even think about exams – you'll come back to it refreshed.

- Take a 5- or 10-minute break every hour, and do some stretching exercises, go for a short walk or make a drink.

- Talk to your family or a friend about your revision – they may be able to help you. For example, they could test you on key facts.

- Keep bullet points on 'crib cards' highlighting important revision points. For example, you could have a list or a mind map of the reasons why Mussolini came to power in 1922. Use these for quick revision and for reading during 'dead' times – when you're waiting for a bus, for example.

- Use mnemonics. This is when you take the first letter of a series of words you want to remember and then make a new sentence. A common mnemonic for remembering the order of the points of the compass (North, East, South and West) is 'Naughty Elephants Squirt Water'. You could use a mnemonic to help you remember the reasons for the rise of fascism in the years 1919–22.

- Some people revise well by listening, so you could try 'talking' your revision and recording it onto an mp3 player if you have one. Listen to these while lying in bed, while travelling in a car or walking to the shops. This also takes the guilt out of being out and about rather than in front of your books!

- Practise your exam techniques. As you revise key topics, plan five or six points to make about the causes/consequences/key features/changes relating to major developments. You could use question stems 1–4 on the previous page, and slot in your own x and y.

- Try doing some timed essays. This will make it easier to write a good essay when it comes to the exam.

- Don't panic. Think about what you can achieve, not what you can't. Positive thinking is important! Remember, the examiner will be looking to reward you for what you can do.

Assessment objectives

To do well in your exam, you need to make sure you meet all the assessment objectives. Below are the assessment objectives you need to meet and some advice on how to make sure you meet them.

Recall, select and deploy historical knowledge

AO1a

In your essay, you must show that you can remember, choose and use historical knowledge.

- Remember – *recollect historical facts from your study of this unit*
- Choose – *select specific facts that are relevant to the essay you are writing*
- Use – *place these facts in your essay in a way that supports your argument*

Understanding of the past

AO1b (i)

You need to show that you understand the period studied. Simply telling the story of what happened will not help you to do this. Instead, you need to:

- Analyse – *break down the topic you are considering into key points*
- Explain – *suggest reasons why these key points provide an answer to the question*
- Reach a judgment – *decide which of your key points was most important and provide reasons to support this*

As you think about analysis, explanation and judgment, remember to bear in mind the relevant **key concepts** and **relationships**.

Key concepts

AO1b (ii)

When faced with an essay question, consider which of the following key concepts it focuses on:

- Causation – *what made an event happen?*
- Consequence – *what were the results of this event?*
- Continuity – *in what ways did things stay the same?*
- Change – *in what ways were things different?*
- Significance – *why was this important?*

Then ensure that your answer remains focused on this concept.

Relationships

AO1b (iii)

Once you have planned the key points you will make in your essay, consider the following:

- How do these key points link together?
- Which key point was most important? Why?

Once you have considered these issues, arrange your points in an order that reflects the way they link together or the relative importance of each key point.

Level descriptors

Each essay you write in the exam will be given a mark out of 30 and will correspond to a level from 1 to 5, with Level 5 being the highest. Here is some information about what the levels mean. Read it carefully and use this information to aim for the top!

Level 1:
- General points about the historical period that are correct but not necessarily focused on the topic raised by the question.
- The general points will not be supported by accurate and relevant specific examples.

Answers at this level will be very simplistic, irrelevant or vague.

Level 2:
- A number of general points about the topic of the question.
- The general points will be supported by some accurate and relevant examples.

Answers at this level might tell the story or part of the story without addressing the question, or might list the key points without backing them up with specific examples.

Level 3:
- A number of points with some focus on the question.
- The points will be supported by accurate material, but some whole paragraphs may be either only partly relevant, lacking in detail or both.

At Level 3 answers will attempt to focus on the question and have some strengths (some paragraphs will have point, supporting evidence and linkage back to the question), but answers will also have significant areas of weakness. For example, the focus on the question may drift, the answer may lack specific examples or parts of the essay may simply tell the story.

Level 4:
- A number of points which clearly address the question and show an understanding of the most important factors involved.
- The points will be supported by accurate material which will be mostly relevant and detailed.
- There will be clear explanation of how the points and specific examples provide an answer to the question.

At Level 4 answers will clearly attempt to tackle the question and demonstrate a detailed knowledge of the period studied.

Level 5:
- A number of points which clearly address the question and show a thorough understanding of the most important factors involved.
- The points will be supported by accurate material which will be relevant and detailed.
- There will be clear explanation of how the points and specific examples provide an answer to the question, as well as an evaluation of the relative importance of the different factors or issues discussed.

Answers that are judged to be Level 5 will be thorough and detailed – they will clearly engage with the specific question, providing a balanced and carefully reasoned argument that reaches a clear and supported judgment.

Sample answer

To what extent did Mussolini's dictatorship rely on repression in the years 1925–43?

An answer given a mark in Level 3 of the published mark scheme

Mussolini became dictator of Italy in 1925–26 after being made prime minister in 1922. Historians are divided over whether Mussolini's regime was repressive or not. He certainly set up the secret police known as OVRA to force people to do what he wanted but he also had to get the agreement of the other parties who served in his coalition. In this essay, I will discuss how far Mussolini's dictatorship relied on repression and how far it didn't.

EXAMINER COMMENT

This is not a particularly good introduction. The candidate provides a relevant piece of information about the OVRA but then makes a point about Mussolini's pre-1925 coalition government which lies outside the period stipulated by the question. The introduction concludes simply by stating the purpose of the essay rather than the judgment it will reach.

During Mussolini's years in power, the Italian people were oppressed by the Fascist regime. Many well-known opponents such as Nitti became 'outsiders'. They fled abroad either to escape Fascist persecution or to protest against the regime. Some of these 'outsiders', including the Rosselli brothers, were tracked down and killed on the Fascist government's orders. The anti-fascist organisation, Justice and Liberty, also challenged Mussolini's dictatorship. It was founded in 1929 and appealed to intellectuals, democrats, socialists, republicans and other opponents. Justice and Liberty developed an underground network and, by the 1930s, was about the size of the PCI.

Inside Italy, the Duce used the OVRA, the secret police force set up in 1926, to try and make sure Italians obeyed the regime. Mussolini liked the name because he thought it sounded sinister. The organisation carried out 20,000 raids a week and had a network of 100,000 informants. It gathered information, and reported on, all aspects of Italian life. Yet, OVRA was not large - in the 1930s it had about 700 agents under the command of Arturo Bocchini, the Fascist chief of police. Most of the people arrested by the secret police were communists and members of Justice and Liberty but few of those who were detained were sent to prison.

EXAMINER COMMENT

In both of these paragraphs, the candidate has introduced some relevant information and has provided some detailed examples. However, both paragraphs lack a clear focus on the question. OVRA is described, but its importance for the regime is not assessed.

Another instrument of repression was the Special Tribunal, a sort of military court, which was set up to try political opponents. The most prominent case for the tribunal involved the leading communist Antonio Gramsci who was given a 20 year prison sentence. From 1926 political prisoners could also be sent into internal exile, known as confino, in remote provinces and islands such as Lipari. Italians could be banished in this way simply because the authorities suspected they were contemplating action against the dictatorship.

EXAMINER COMMENT

This paragraph focuses on the question but offers very limited specific information to support its points. It does not consider the extent to which the Special Tribunal and confino were used as instruments of repression.

The regime, however, did not rely entirely on repression. Mussolini also tried to persuade Italians to accept the Fascist system through various propaganda measures. Fascist censorship of the press was designed to portray the system in the best possible light. Perhaps the most important propaganda device to generate popular support was the cult of the Duce which claimed that Mussolini was an infallible and supremely gifted leader.

EXAMINER COMMENT

This paragraph also focuses well on the question by challenging the view that the regime relied heavily on repression. However, although the points made about propaganda and persuasion are relevant, they are very general and are not supported with specific information.

Overall, I feel that Mussolini's dictatorship did rely on repression because he used the OVRA and the Special Tribunal to ensure political opponents could not challenge his power. Having said this, the regime also used propaganda in an attempt to convince Italians of the benefits of fascism.

EXAMINER COMMENT

This response was awarded a mark in Level 3 of the mark scheme [13–18 marks]. The candidate clearly has some understanding of the requirements of the question. However, none of the paragraphs meet all of these requirements. In the earlier paragraphs, the candidate displays detailed knowledge without a precise focus on the question. In the later paragraphs, the focus improves but the level of detail drops. Due to the fact that the essay covers a good range of relevant factors, and that there is some detail and some focus, it meets the criteria for high Level 3 and was given 17 marks.

Index

Published by Pearson Education Limited, a company incorporated in England and Wales, having its registered office at Edinburgh Gate, Harlow, Essex, CM20 2JE. Registered company number: 872828

www.pearsonschoolsandfecolleges.co.uk

Edexcel is a registered trademark of Edexcel Limited

Text © Pearson Education Limited 2011

First published 2011

13 12 11

10 9 8 7 6 5 4 3 2 1

British Library Cataloguing in Publication Data

A catalogue record for this book is available from the British Library.

ISBN 978 1 84690 750 0

Edited by Polly Hennessy
Typeset by Ian Foulis
Original illustrations © Pearson Education 2010
Illustrated by Ian Foulis
Printed and bound at Henry Ling, Dorset, UK

Acknowledgements

The author and publisher would like to thank the following individuals and organisations for permission to reproduce photographs:
(Key: b-bottom; c-centre; l-left; r-right; t-top)

Alamy Images: Photos 9, 24, Trinity Mirror / Mirrorpix 27; **Alinari Archives Management, Florence:** Bruni Archive / Alinari Archives Management, Florence 64, Fratelli Alinari Museum Collections-Malandrini Collection, Florence 25, **Fratelli Alinari Museum Collections, Florence** 40; **BPK:** Bayerische Staatsbibliothek | Heinrich Hoffmann 70; **Bridgeman Art Library Ltd:** Giuseppe Pellizza da Volpedo 17; **Corbis:** Bettmann 48, 68, Hulton-Deutsch Collection 35; **Fiat Group:** 16; **Getty Images:** AFP 58, Topical Press Agency 56, Lambert 80, Popperfoto 101; **Kobal Collection Ltd:** Achille Beltrame / Domenica del Corriere 69; **Solo Syndication/ Associated Newspapers Ltd:** David Low, Evening Standard / British Cartoon Archive, University of Kent www.cartoons.ac.uk 105; **TopFoto:** 108, Ullsteinbild 100

Cover images: *Front:* **TopFoto:** FotoWare Foto Station

The author and publisher would like to thank the following individuals and organisations for permission to reproduce copyrighted material:

Figures

Figure in unit 1 adapted from 'The Italian Front 1915-1918' from *Recent History Atlas*, Weidenfeld and Nicolson (Gilbert, M., 1966) p.29. Reproduced with permission of A P Watt Ltd on behalf of The Right Honourable Sir Martin Gilbert OBE.

Tables

Table in unit 8 from *Italian Fascism: Its Origins and Development*, University of Nebraska Press (Alexander De Grand) p.63, by permission of the University of Nebraska Press. Copyright 1982, 1989, 2000 by the University of Nebraska Press; Table in unit 10 from *The Italian Navy and Fascist Expansionism*, 1935-40, Cass Publishing (Mallet, R., 1998) pp.601, 935-940. Reproduced by permission of Taylor & Francis Books.

Every effort has been made to contact copyright holders of material reproduced in this book. Any omissions will be rectified in subsequent printings if notice is given to the publishers. In some instances we have been unable to trace the owners of copyright material, and we would appreciate any information that would enable us to do so.